Into the Dragon's Roar

by Don Arndt

ISBN 978-1-300-49882-7

www.seethedragon.com

About the cover

I took this photo as we worked our way across the lands of Vietnam. We were close to a place called Ho Bo woods. Bill Franklin is right in front of me, then Joey Barresi and Sgt Randle.

Dedication

I was thinking I needed to dedicate this to more than one group, or maybe to the two Battalions of Wolfhounds. But there were so many valorous units that paid such a price. And then I considered maybe more than one man, but I wouldn't know where to stop. So many gave so much! I have decided to dedicate these stories to my best friend of my life, Charlie Crowe. Charlie died in Vietnam July 16, 1966 and I think of him every day. I'll let this dedication to him stand for all the 58,000 plus soldiers that gave all they had so long ago.

I was 50 yards from Charlie when he got hurt and then he died three days later. I never got to say good bye to Charlie until 16 years later when I stood beside his grave in the hills of Tennessee and I cried. How he loved those old rolling hills and his farm.

Table of Contents

Preface

There are tens of thousands stories out there that should be told. To give you somewhat of an idea of how many stories are out there that need to be told, one needs to get some concept of the magnitude of the Vietnam War in numbers you can understand. I know terms like Divisions, Battalions and Regiments, etc., are confusing to non-veterans and even Military service veterans other than Army veterans as other terms are used of course. So, if over 550,000 military in Vietnam at the height of the War and the tours were usually one year, the numbers become almost unbelievably large for this very long war.

With that in mind, the 27th Infantry Regiment (called the Wolfhounds) who nearly all this book is written about is only one Regiment, one part of the 25th Division. A Division being made up of many Regiments was then about 10,000 soldiers at any one time.

Now that all that is clear, the next numbers will make sense and should shake you. The 25th Division lost 4,240 men in the four years they were in Vietnam. Killed. That is Four Thousand two hundred forty young men KIA, just in our Division alone. Along with that, the Division also had 30,000 men wounded. Every one of those that died had a best friend that still suffers from the loss. Every single one of these best friends and every one of these 30,000 wounded have stories locked away somewhere in their minds that should be told. It's a shame, but most will never be told. The names, deeds and memories of those thousands of brave Americans will someday be buried with their best friends, their "brothers." (Stats from *Red Thunder, Tropic Lightning: The World of a Combat Division in Vietnam* By Eric Bergerud.)

These will be but just a few of those stories from a select group of my friends. These are stories of men that walked and they ran and then they rode and of course, sometimes they flew *Into the Dragon's Roar.* None fled from that horrible roar. None left that roar until the dragon was quiet once again.

Introduction

My first book published in late 2007, *See the Dragon,* was mostly my story with a few stories of my closest friends included. It was mainly how being with those I served with changed my life. I wanted my grandkids to "know" those wonderful, amazing and very brave men I had spent a tour in Vietnam with. Their stories were from my view point, not theirs.

I'll explain where the title of my first book came from. To "See the Dragon" meant to be in the mix… the battle. Meaning that a full bore all-out battle sounds like nothing most people have ever heard. But we imagined the roar of a dragon. It might just sound like that. Where the individual small arms rounds were not distinguishable, but were a solid deafening loud roar.

That book was never written with the intent to become published. It was indeed a letter to my grandchildren so, some day they would "know" who their grandpa was. I wanted them to always remember the names of the heroes I served with in the Army and especially the names of my buddies that were lost in Vietnam.

It was very important to me that those fine young men's sacrifices and short lives stay in someone's memory after I was gone.

This writing is different in that I am writing it with the full intention of this one being published someday and be somewhat of a tiny history of my unit while they served in the Vietnam War. This project will not be much of my story, but will include stories of other members of the famous Wolfhounds. I will comment on some of them as they tell their respective tales of humor… and terror… and simply finding a way to live through a tour of a nightmare. There will be a few exceptions, because the Wolfhounds worked closely with other units of the 25th Division, and even other Divisions such as the valorous First Division known as the Big Red One. I have many friends from my home town that served in Vietnam that were members of other units too, and I feel I need to include some of their "best" experiences.

I am going to steal three or four chapters from *See the Dragon* and stick them in here as they need to be included. Maybe I should have called this simply a sequel to the first book.

All of these stories are from men I know. Some are those that I was with and watched grow into men back in 1965 and '66 and some are those that were in my unit that I never really met for the first time until we talked at one of our reunions.

Because of *See the Dragon*, I have met or had phone conversations with hundreds of Wolfhounds from all over the Nation. Because of the "Dragon," I have been asked to speak at various functions and gatherings where I have met many more veterans with amazing tales of tremendous valor, some of humor, and some, of course, just plain silliness.

All these encounters have one thing in common. With almost no exception, the stories of valor are told of a buddy, not of themselves. Every medal winner I visited with was reluctant to tell “his” story, but wanted to relay what he had seen his buddy do. They usually say they didn’t do anything anyone else wouldn’t do, and they were only doing their job. Such fine men all.

Dwight D. Eisenhower was a great General, maybe one of the finest. Certainly in World War II he stood tall among the tallest. I admire his service greatly and many of his quotes I love. I disagree with him on one big one however. As the invasion of Europe was beginning he said, “I feel we’ll never see the likes of men like these again”. How wrong he was! In Korea, Vietnam, Iraq and Afghanistan we called on American men and women again and again and always we found the same soldiers as General Eisenhower found in his time. There is no difference in these Americans serving and those of sixty years ago, only different enemies. There are millions of stories out there that need to be told, from Pusan, Korea to Baghdad. Millions of Americans served in hundreds of units, each with stories to tell.

As you read the following accounts and feelings of my friends, pay particular attention to a couple of men’s stories. One is Bob Park’s contribution. Bob not only shares some interesting events with us, but he does something that most can’t seem to do. He puts into words his innermost feeling of the heart about his time in Vietnam. We all were devoted to our buddies and Bob Park is able to come pretty close to putting into words the love of the brothers we had… and have still today. Also read Matthew Kritzer's heartfelt description of of his feelings of losing his best friend. I lost my best friend there and I have several friends that suffered that loss also, but Matthew is able to put into very descriptive words what so many feel and cannot explain.

These will be but a few stories, mostly from men from a small unit known as the Wolfhounds. As the reader works their way through these pages, as they get to "know" the men (I should say boys), I want them to really stop once in a while, just pause and think of what these men each gave. Ponder on what horror they each endured and what things they saw. Imagine the heat and the rain and the nights and the misery that they worked in every day. Then notice how they don't dwell on that, instead they continue moving their story to the others… their buddies, yes their "brothers". That is where their heart is. That is where their memories take them in the night. That is where they are when they seem to stare at nothing for no reason, that's where. In those strange times, those staring times, they are with those men they knew and just for a little while, maybe they are with those that they saw die.

My story

Before I get much deeper in this project, I should let you understand a little of who I am.

I was raised on a small farm in western Missouri and was drafted into the Army April of 1965. I was a simple rural kid that knew nothing of the world outside my township. The only things I knew about were cattle, machinery and engines. When I received my draft notice I was 22 years old and working for the Chevrolet Dealership in Drexel, Mo as a mechanic and was also farming my place nights and weekends. I consider myself to be one of the luckiest guys to serve in Vietnam for several reasons.

First of all, I was sent to Hawaii and joined a unit that was training hard and then that unit went to Vietnam together like a great big team. I wasn't a replacement like the thousands that went after me. Being with the guys you had been training with for 5 or 6 months was such a comfort.

Second, many of the people that served in any of the services will tell of guys they were with that were a mix of nice guys, show offs, thieves, jerks, slackers and heroes. For some reason that God only knows why I was allowed to be with only the good. Men you would want to be with. It was almost like I was allowed to pick them. Also for the most part, we had fine, capable officers and non-coms. If any drugs were taken in my unit, I never knew of it. There was lots of beer of course, but no one "worked" drunk that I ever saw.

I felt like I had joined a unit above me, kinda like when a guy says he "married up," I guess I was "assigned up." I think I was a good soldier, but I'm sure I contributed little to the effort at hand even though I did everything I was told as best I could. Many of my friends "made a difference" and I saw many acts that made me proud to be with them.

I listened to griping everyday about the heat, bad food, sleeping on the ground and in the rainy season I heard all the complaints about that. I was one of the best of the groaners about those things. But never did I hear anyone bad mouth our country. I never heard anyone go off on being caught up in a mess that we shouldn't be in. I guess being in the very earliest part of the war we just thought it was our duty and we did our job.

I saw many men cry, but not for themselves and their predicament. No, it was always for a buddy hurt or lost or maybe seeing a baby killed or civilian family lost for no reason. I have believed ever since the war that the man I became was mostly due to the men I learned to love like brothers. I gained so much strength from just working with these men.

Stats

I won’t be putting any more statistics (courtesy of the VFW magazine) down after these few comments in this short paragraph. The intent here in the following pages is to tell of the personal trials and just a little history on a soldier level and not trying to make any kind of political statement. Stories of these patriots need to be recorded as soon as possible because of the 2.7 million that served in Vietnam, only about one third still live in 2012.

I read in the veteran’s magazine about an estimate that one of every ten that served in Vietnam was a casualty. There were 997 KIA their first day in country! There were 1448 killed on their last day of the yearlong tour.

Those soldiers that served during the long and terrible WWII had a bad time and I don’t intend to take away from their great sacrifice or those that followed during the Korean War by repeating the following fact. During WWII the average soldier saw 40 days of combat during the four years. The average soldier in Vietnam saw 240 days of combat in his one year tour.

Vietnam Vets have had a bad case of media and Hollywood misinformation ever since the War. The image of the homeless, begging and unemployed man in his fatigue jacket has been the norm on TV. The fact is Vietnam Veterans have a lower unemployment rate than their same age non-vet counterparts. Ok, I’ve got those few stats out of the way.

The Wolfhounds

Only the two Battalions of the 27th Infantry Regiment of the 25th Division are known as “Wolfhounds”. About 600 soldiers make up a Battalion, so at any given time there should be about 1200 soldiers in the United States Army that are called the “Wolfhounds”.

I think a brief history of the Wolfhounds is in order before we get very far into this little history lesson.

The regiment was organized by an Act of Congress on February 2, 1901 making it the oldest Regiment in the US Army. You will find that the Wolfhound Spirit was alive and well from the first day of the unit. The story of the “Wolfhounds” covers more than one hundred years of service to the United States, from the Philippine Insurrection, to Siberia, throughout the Pacific, Korea, Vietnam, Afghanistan, and Iraq. Early in their history that they received their “nickname.” And almost unbelievably, that nickname came from a Russian. After seeing the 27th Infantry in battle in the early 1900’s, a Russian General said to the Regiment’s Commander that his men fought like a Russian wolfhound and promptly presented the Commander a gift of one of the famous dogs. The dog’s name was Kolchak. Since that day, there has been a Russian wolfhound living at Schofield barracks on the island of Oahu, Hawaii. When the K9 is lost due to old age or illness, another dog is found and a number is added to his name. When I was stationed there in 1965, I believe we had Kolchak V and he was billeted in a nice big cage/home in the middle of our quadrant. He was pampered beyond belief. He was coddled and loved like you would a little brother. Today that tradition goes on and there living at Schofield Barracks today is a Kolchak number something or other.

Over the years there have been 14 Wolfhound Medal of Honor recipients and many of its officers have gone on to make General. The Regiment has a reputation of utter ferocity in combat and gentle compassion in peace. Our enemies have felt the ruthlessness of the Wolfhound's bite, our friends have found us to be loyal and steadfast, and the innocent have found the Wolfhounds are second to none in compassion.

The Wolfhounds association with the Holy Family Home in Japan has gone on since the occupation of Japan after World War II. During the occupation of Japan right after the end of World War II, Wolfhound Sergeant O'Reilly found an orphanage among the rubble with several children being taken care of by a few nuns and one older lady in particular. He found they had little food, clothing and other necessities of life. Within weeks he had rallied his fellow Wolfhounds to volunteer supplies and much needed help to the kids. This soon became a tradition ingrained into the very heart of the Regiment that stands today. One of the first things I found after I arrived in Hawaii in August of 1965 was the fact that everyone wearing the Wolfhound crest gave at least one dollar of his pay each payday to the orphanage fund. I was told it was not mandatory, "BUT", the old Wolfhound officer says to me, "until right now they have always been 100% volunteering that dollar. Now you don't want to be the one to break that?" I sure didn't!

Every summer several children from the orphanage visit the regiment in Hawaii, and every December, two Wolfhound soldiers visit Osaka, Japan bearing gifts for each of the children as our very own Santa-Ambassadors.

There is a movie, vintage about 1955, which tells the tale of the "Holy Family" Orphanage. The name of the movie is "Three Stripes in the Sun". I love the old black and white movie that tells the story of Sgt O'Rielly and his fellows Wolfhounds founding that orphanage. Sgt Hugh O'Rielly married a Japanese national lady named Yuko and they were together until his death in June of 2006. The old Sgt was 91 years old.

I have read several books in my life and not once have I written to or looked up a phone number and called an author. Never. I didn't even know it was ever done. A lot of these stories will get their beginning from just such calls to me about my book, *See the Dragon*. Now I don't have any thought that that book was well written, in fact, I always thought I should have a professional writer rewrite the thing after I was talked into publishing it. I say this to make it clear that the boat load of phone calls that I got about the book was due to the fact that I brought back memories to some veterans and they wanted to talk to me about it. It had nothing to do with the quality of the writings. I've said many, many times that the book was nothing at all compared to what the book has done since. Many of the following stories would never have been brought to light had it not been for the "Dragon". Also, of the hundreds of calls, not one has been a bad experience. I wouldn't take anything for any of the conversations, not anything. I have met some of the most interesting people and heard the most uplifting testimonies imaginable. I have now personally met, visited with and taken meals with many of them that before the phone call were total strangers.

I know now that the bond that is forged between soldiers that served together is not the only bond that can't really be properly described. There is also something strong, something magnetic, some unseen tie between Vietnam veterans. It is a closeness that I can't put words down that will make anyone understand, but all veterans understand without question.

I still intend for this to be mainly stories about Wolfhounds, but there have been so many veterans and family of veterans call me with their stories that I feel I must share some of them. I am more sure now than ever, that the news media in the 60's were very close to being criminal with their terrible slant. After getting to know so many veterans and the lives they led after the war, it is clear to me that Hollywood was as wrong as the media. Few of the veterans I've talked to had a problem with finding a good life. Nearly all are Christians, all but a few were extremely successful, hardworking family men and women. Many of them have enjoyed long term marriages and raised amazing families. Certainly a far cry from the picture that has been painted of the vet standing on the corner wearing the fatigue jacket, drunk and begging.

Another thing I found was that nearly all were "closet" Vietnam veterans for 35 or 38 years. That was me of course. I received many calls from family members of veterans telling me that "their" vet had never or seldom mentioned the war. I have had young folks ask me how to get their dad to tell them about it. Of course, I have no answer for that. Usually a reunion with the old unit of some kind will shake them into telling their story. Just a meeting of one of the guys they served with will sometimes do it.

When I visit with siblings and children of Vietnam vets and their wives also, the first and certainly most common comment I hear goes something like this; "But he never talked about the war" or "He has said so little about it all the many years I've been with him". I've heard many times that the first time a wife heard about anything from his experiences was after he attended a reunion or after he read my first book.

Please don't think of this as a collection of war stories. These are people stories…boys turning into men stories. These are hero stories and friendship stories and losing brothers stories. These are the stories about the lives that the sons of mothers endured. These are stories that were happening while mothers wrung their hands and cried back home and their fathers cried in secret. Some are tales of great valor and some are just sad, but all are real.

66 Day Battle for Cu Chi

I was stationed at Schofield Barracks in Oahu, Hawaii for the last half of 1965, then during late December the 25th Division was ordered to the new conflict in Vietnam. We were transported to Vietnam by two troop ships, the USS General Gordon and the one I was on, the USS General Walker.

I think we landed on the shores of Vietnam Jan 16th of 1966. I still remember the first time the smell of Vietnam hit me. I won't try to describe it because I can't. Spending all of my 21 years on a farm I thought I had experienced every smell and mixtures of smells known to mankind. I was wrong. The first few weeks in country had been nothing short of organized chaos and I think the brass just wanted time to settle down. I'm sure it didn't seem all messed up to the brass, but to a simple farm boy with one PFC stripe it was very overwhelming to say the least. With no base camp, we were sent somewhere to guard an airfield for what seemed like a week or two. Later we learned that our leaders were picking a place to build a permanent camp site. The Cu Chi site was chosen because the water table was deeper there than anywhere and plans were to bring in armor soon. Armor would not be good during the monsoon with a water table at surface level. Everything would have sunk.

I learned about those decisions a few years ago while reading about the life of General Fred C Weyand who was our division commander. General Weyand was probably the single sharpest of all the Generals during the Vietnam War.

In just a few days we commenced to take this special land away from the Communists. This was to inflict a big psychological blow to the enemy. The 5000 troops of the 25th were able to take the base camp, but it cost a great deal. I watched a documentary on TV where they said when the 25th Division took Cu Chi we had 8000 men. We always thought we were 5000. I'm sure the TV show is right. We now owned what later became known as the Cu Chi base camp. It was named that because of the little Village that was situated a few clicks from the camp. By this time it was February or March of 1966 and still very hot and every unit was sending out LP's (Listening Posts) at night. The enemy probed the base every little bit and hit us with rocket and mortar fire.

The main reason, however, that taking this area away from Charlie (the Viet Cong) turned out to be a bad idea, is the fact that while Charlie had the place for his home he had dug an underground city directly under it. The entire year that I was there we never had a truly secure camp. Now, this idea of picking the Cu Chi area for the new giant 25th Division base camp was no one's fault. The brass simply didn't know the enemy was below the whole area. Who would have? It was many years after that the true extent and sheer magnitude of the tunnels came to light. The

VC came up out of the holes and climbed into trees and hid in little camouflaged areas so they could snipe us. The camp was almost totally grown up with foliage. When we first got in there, it was nothing but a jungle and we spent a lot of our days, while in the area, cutting trees and underbrush. Each squad was expanding their own area.

Here is Harold “Monty” Montgomery with our “barracks” at Cu Chi base camp early in 1966. Monty was in Hawaii with us and rode the USS General Walker with the rest of the Division. Monty was married at the time and I believe the married guys suffered much more than the rest of us.

We made our shelters out of ponchos put up on bamboo sticks. That worked real well too. Being settled into one area for a home base was great, as now we could get our fox holes deeper and wider. I remember the outer perimeter of our 25th Division was a single roll of concertina wire and that was several days after we were settled in. Still no rain and it was becoming more dusty by the day. The heat was still a factor and it never cooled all year. We had holes dug every few feet all the way around the compound and each hole had three men with it. Everybody pulled perimeter duty. At night there was always at least one awake and two asleep in each hole during the night. We were sending more patrols out at this time so there were some of our people in the bush night and day. Most of the Wolfhound's operations were company size. (100 plus) and several became battalion size missions (400 to 500 men).

By March and April the camp looked much different, but we continued to be plagued by snipers every day inside the camp plus the enemy tried frontal assaults along with mortar and rocket attacks often. The snipers were mostly for psychological damage. We did loose people from them of course, but the knowledge of them being there and could pop a round at any time weighed on our minds constantly. We would figure out which tree he was in, but even after you hit him, the fear was still there because they would not fall out of the tree. The Viet Cong would tie themselves and their weapon to the tree so we would not be sure if we got him or not. This was to mess with our minds too. It worked.

Nearly a year earlier at Fort Leonard Wood I had made a decision to turn down going to OCS and becoming an officer. I was now feeling really good about that decision shortly after I was inducted. We had taken a few rounds of tests in Ft Leonard Wood, Mo before basic started. After a while, me and two other guys were called into a special room. We were told we were going to go to OCS. Of course none of us had a clue what that was and after he explained I said no, and asked what other choices there were. He said if we didn't do OCS we had to do a 5 week non-com leadership school. We all three took the non com deal. After the short "special" basic training we took real eight week basic with a regular company then. I was already being screwed with and I had been a soldier for 10 seconds. Now, more than ever, just wanted to do my two years and get back to my life. I missed the farm; I missed the smell of the hay barn and fried chicken and cold winter mornings. Yes, cold winter mornings on the farm have a very special smell too!

I always wondered if I would have been able to "cut it" as an officer especially here in a combat situation. The huge responsibility of being an officer would have weighed on this old farm boy terribly I'm sure. This way, the number of people I was concerned and worried about was limited to myself, my buddies and and my widowed mother back home. At the time of my induction I was full support of my mom on that small mid west farm. My dad had died of a heart attack when I was 14, so I had taken over the farm at that time. I constantly worried how she would make it with out me. Well, this being a regular soldier with very little rank was better than being "in charge" for me because I wouldn't ever make a decision and put out orders that might get people hurt. I would do my best and do what I was told at the best of my ability.

So here I was in Vietnam in March of 1966. The 25th Division's "Command Group" arrived and that changed everything to a little more organized and military like. The 66 day running Battle for CU CHI earned the Division another "Presidential Unit Citation" and is where I and most of my buddies was awarded our CIBs.

Stories of My Brothers

I believe this should be the first story I tell about because it really hits the nail on the head with what I'm trying to do here. This is a case of "small world" at its best and will sort of make you think that some of these reunions are just "supposed to happen". This is the story of one of my Vietnam buddies; this is a real good friend that I had not seen for about 45 years.

Paul Wells. Fayette, Missouri: Farm Boy

Paul Wells

It was 8:30 in the PM, April 1st 2009. I was thinking about going to bed and the phone rang. Sue answered and I heard her say, “Sure, he’s right here”.

The call started like so many had. The man on the phone said he had my book on his lap and then was silent. I said “I hope you liked it”. He said “Oh, I haven’t read it yet.” I noted a little emotional tone here, “I’ve only had your book for 20 minutes now. I only looked at a couple of pictures and had to call you. I got your number from information.” Then he asked, “So, Don, how have you been?” I thought that that was a strange thing to say since this guy don’t know me and he hasn’t even read about me or my buddies yet. After some more silence he then said, “Don, this is Paul Wells.” I couldn’t believe it. This guy was a buddy from Vietnam forty three years ago. We talked for an hour and barely just scratched the surface of what each had been up too. That usually takes days to catch up. But, the way he found me and how this came to be is the amazing part of this story.

My son in law John George, lives in Columbia Missouri and has worked for the Missouri Conservation Dept for many years. One of his co-workers is a young lady that has worked there for eight years. They have talked many times about her father being a Vietnam vet and never talking about his service and John’s father in law (Me) who had written a book about his time there. Just by chance on April 1st, John asked her if she thought her daddy would read my book. She thought it was worth a try and borrowed it. That night she drove to her dad’s house, got there at eight o’clock and handed it to him.

Now, I got this next part from my son in law John. Her daddy turned a funny color, looked at it a bit and said, I have to call this guy and went to the phone. Evidently while he was doing this he pointed at my name on the front of the book and told her that this guy was his sergeant and had saved his life. This is where forty three year old memories get pretty foggy. I know I wasn't a Sergeant and it is doubtful I had much to do with saving his life, unless I took some C rations away from him that would have killed him. He thought I was his sergeant and that's OK. I was really an E 4 at the time, but was indeed his boss (for a little while). That's another story. We agreed that we had to get together soon and began to lay plans.

I talked with him a couple of days later and the first thing he said was he had read the book and that I had named it wrong. He claimed I should have called it "the Onion Book". "What?" I say to him. He said it was because every time he picks it up he starts crying. Now, it's not because "See The Dragon" is a sad book. I think men cry because when they read it and other books it causes them to remember friends lost and a youth spent in a very bad place. They remember the time spent learning about death and certainly about life and how fragile and important it is. The time they lost when most young people were learning things that teens are supposed to be learning and laughing and dancing and loving.

Sue and I drove to somewhere way out in the back country north of a town called Boonesboro (wasn't on the map) Missouri for visit. If it had not been for cell phones we would have never found them. We got a great meal out of it. Wanda, his wonderful wife of 43 years, can really cook. They are retired, living on their farm, got seven grandkids and happy as larks in a tree. We looked at pictures and lots of mementoes, explored his barn full of antique restored tractors and motorized toys he's built for the kids (Looks just like my place) and generally had a great time. We were getting together again soon. Absolutely.

So, now about Paul and Vietnam. Some of this I don't remember, but Paul filled in the blanks pretty well for me. John Puffenburger was my squad leader and sometime around May or early June of 1966, he spent six weeks in a Japan hospital getting repaired. While he was gone, little ol' Spec 4 me was the boss guy. Captain Bryant told me to go up to the division replacement area and grab some new-be (called FNG's) to help me, just a body to fill in a slot. I'm not sure exactly the criteria I asked when I went for this replacement. I think I asked if anyone there was a Missouri farm boy and Paul raised his hand. Paul remembers the odd ordeal differently. I imagine the truth lies somewhere in between. I ask him if he wanted to work with us and he did. He was a great guy and when John Puffenburger came back, we kept Paul with us. I left Vietnam the last day of December or the 1st of

January 1967 and Paul, of course, had to stay 6 more months in Vietnam for his full year. However we came to have this man, we were the winners. He was a great guy and even if he was a replacement, we got to know him well. We became quick friends with a lot in common, so when he and his wife Wanda lost their baby, it shook us all. The whole platoon wrote a condolence letter and scraped up a few dollars to send to her. Paul was able to get a short emergency leave to go be with his wife.

While Sue and I were at their home April 8th 2009 for that visit, Wanda brought out some of her mementos and showed us the card we had sent her during her "hard time" with all of our 27 signatures of the platoon on it. Then, Paul and Wanda said at the same time, "There was $80.00 tucked inside it."

Paul and Wanda Wells made it to the 2010 Wolfhound reunion in Branson, MO and what a great reunion it was. Larry 'Deacon' Brown, Bill Franklin, Paul Wells, myself and Patsy Clayton, the sister of our friend Charlie Crowe (KIA July 16th, 1966), were all together.

Elmer "Em" French, Marion, Ohio: A Really Big Man

Elmer French (left) and Don Arndt

I probably knew Em as well as I ever knew anyone. We were together seventeen months total. Five months in Hawaii and then the year in Nam.

Elmer French, now he was from Marion, Ohio and not a very big kid. We called him Em. He only weighed about 100 lbs soaking wet. If I had to describe Em with only one word it would probably be "intelligent". He was a super guy to be with and there really were no dull moments if you were around him. He was a very mischievous soldier with a huge dislike of officers. Elmer was the biggest little man I ever knew. I never saw a hint of fear in the man all the time I knew him. He was one of the few guys that were married and he called his wife "Mouse". They had a little girl named Connie and he was so lonely for them and you could always see the hurt in his face. I was glad I was not married because the married guys always had a lot rougher time of it as they worried about their families, but we were responsible for only ourselves.

Elmer was in Hawaii when I got there and we ended up together for 17 months Elmer was kind of a self-appointed cook for us. In Vietnam he would take rations from several men and dump each of their can of the main course in his helmet, mix it up, and heat it. I remember if you had "drawn" a C ration containing the pork, you were not included in Em's food party. He claimed the pork had too much salt and would ruin his concoction. That was a great rule if you were lucky enough to draw the right C's. When he was finished with adding spices and junk, everyone that had contributed, dipped up a can of the mix.

Our helmets were in two parts, a liner and the pot (or outer metal). When you pulled the liner out, the helmet made a perfect pot to cook in or to shave with, among other uses. I've sat on mine for many hours and I always shaved out of it. We used Gillette blue blades in a safety razor and those blades would stay sharp for about 2 strokes, then came the pulling. We always shaved in cold water and made lather with soap.

Em had a habit of exclaiming his dislike not only for Officers, but the entire way the Army ran itself. He always called his weapon a gun (a real no-no) and an Army truck or jeep was always called Army cars. To this day, when I see a convoy of Army trucks on the highway, I exclaim "there goes Army cars", and think of Em. I think he might have been in denial of his commitment to the Army, but always remained a perfect soldier. I don't know what drew guys to like Em, but everyone liked him from the first minute they met him. It was probably his "fun at all costs" personality and the fact that he was so much more of a man than he first appeared, because of his small stature. Em always pulled more than his weight and someone I always knew was to be counted on, no matter what. I was a much larger man than Em, but I never had a thought that I could "handle" him if it ever became necessary.

This is the best Elmer story I have. One night, of course it was pitch dark, as there is no electricity on the base, and several of us were sitting around visiting. Elmer had been drinking some beer and sharpening his "chetty" as he called it. Elmer had taken a Machete knife out of one of the houses in a village we had swept through. He spent a lot of time sharpening that thing. Seems as though the officers had got themselves an electric hotplate and light of some sort, hooked it up to a 5 kilo-watt, gasoline powered generator to power it. They were cooking steaks or something,

I’m sure they had forgotten about all of us EM still eating C rations. Officers do stuff like that sometimes. The thing is, the officers did not want the noise of that engine by their area, so they ran a long extension cord down by us and sat the engine down in our area, where all but a few of us were going to get some sleep in a little while. That thing was noisy and the drunker Elmer got, the madder he got. Pretty soon Elmer got up with old “chetty” in hand and disappeared into the darkness. After a short spell, we all heard this loud snap and saw a big flash of light over by the generator set. Elmer, with one powerful stroke, had cut that extension cord. The gen set picked up speed because the load was removed, the officers started yelling, and about then Elmer came back in from the darkness that he had disappeared in. There was a half moon chunk burned out of the blade of “chetty”. Elmer had struck a blow for us EM against our enemy, the officers. He was our hero. The next day repairs were made on the wire, from then on the length cord was a guard post that had to be walked all night by an EM. We still claimed victory over the officers, however.

Nearly everyone had nick names or at least an altered version of their name that they were called. Em tried his best to call me Elk or Missouri Elk, and even wrote it on my helmet cover. But I would always be known as Arnie despite all his efforts. I think it might have been too complicated to stick. He explained that since Missouri has no Elk, (he poked fun of Missouri quite often) then the Missouri mule must be the closest thing for us to an Elk. Just too deep I guess. He should have started calling me Mule. That would have stuck.

I can't tell Elmer stories without including the water buffalo. We were on a company size sweep (about 100 men) and I don't recall where, but we were crossing some dried up rice paddies. One of the many water buffalo that were grazing there evidently didn't like Elmer's looks or his smell, anyway, this cow charged ol' Elmer and some of the fellows yelled at Elmer to look out behind him. He turned around and was looking right at the front end of a crazy buffalo, so Em' ripped about 7 or 8 rounds from his M16 right up the neck and head. That cow rolled forward into a heap. About 3 seconds after the cow fell dead, a local farmer came running toward the scene yelling at the top of his little oriental voice. Our Captain settled him down and then wrote him out a paper that he could take to Saigon to get reimbursed for his animal. We don't know what he was yelling, but odds are it was local talk for something fairly bad. None of us spoke Vietnamese. Elmer always wanted to add the cow to his body count after that. He claimed it was a VC buffalo.

Elmer and I were great friends and had tons of fun in Hawaii. Nam wasn't as much fun, but Em was one of the guys that made the tour bearable for many of us. However bad things got, he could always find a way to make you grin, if just for a while. Em was, and always will be, my brother.

Don and Em after over 45 years separated, together in Marion, Ohio in summer 2012

Bill Franklin, Rolla, Missouri: The Best of the Best

Bill Franklin on the right

I love to hear short stories of goofy things that happen, especially in the Army. While visiting again with Bill Franklin, I got a little more information about his second tour. If you read my book "See the Dragon", you know how much I always admired Bill. He was certainly a soldier's soldier and we served together during his first tour. I always liked to hang close to Bill always hoping his “Lack of fear” would somehow rub off on me. This is one of the stories he told me that I didn't enter in my first book.

In his second tour, Bill was a door gunner on a Huey Slick working with ¾ Cav. This Cav unit is still a part of the mighty 25th Division just not the Wolfhounds. On one particular mission, after taking a lot of fire and returning the same, Bill's communication suddenly stopped. Bill checked to make sure his coiled mic cable was still plugged in above him and it was, so they continued the mission without talking. When they got back to base, the pilot told him that something was really wrong with his helmet. He took it off and saw that a round had passed right above his head and went through the back of his helmet severing his commo cord leaving a tail of it about 10 inches long. The enemy round had passed only about 1/2 inch by his head. Bill put the helmet away to keep for a souvenir of course.

When his rotation date finally came around, he grabbed up all of his junk including his "near miss" helmet and reported to the airfield to depart. He was on the tarmac about to board the plane when the last man to approve his departure stopped him.

This Second Lt jerk says to him, "You got papers for that helmet?"

"No" Bill says, "It's junk as you can see. The whole back of it was shot away. It is my souvenir."

Lt Jerk told him he ain't taking it without papers because it's government property. "Furthermore", he says, "You ain't boarding with it."

After some argument Bill turned around and threw the helmet as hard as he could across the tarmac and told LT that if he needed it so bad to go after it. Bill got on the plane and left to travel home. Bill told me the last thing he saw in Vietnam was that helmet rolling across the tarmac with that piece of cord flopping around every turn.

I asked Bill if he would like to run into that guy someday. He thought he might enjoy that.

Bill and his wife Rosily joined several of us at the 2010 Branson reunion, then late in 2010. Later, Bill drove up to my home and we spend some time together, took in a car race and just visited.

Jim Hauser: Wolfhound

In early November '66, Jim was with company A during the battle at Dau Theing. When they were ambushed and then they turned to regroup, Jim was shot in the chest. He went down as the Medic and their company commander, Captain Foley reached him. Jim tried to tell them something but he couldn't speak. After the medic applied the dressing and pressed on the wound he could get words out. He said "Captain, the SOB's are in the trees too. (Of course he didn't really say SOB) Give me a weapon sir, I've lost mine". Captain Foley reached down and put his hand on Jim's shoulder and told him the war was over for him. The machine gunner had just been killed. Captain Foley then turned, picked up the M 60 machine gun, threw the belt of ammo over his shoulder and charged the enemy bunkers along with John Baker. Jim lay there critically wounded and could only watch as Captain Foley and Baker each earned the Medal of Honor.

Jim recovered from those wounds and is active today in many pro Veteran functions.

Medal of Honor recipient John Baker passed away in 2012.

Related story. At one of our reunions as we were having the annual fund raising auction, the auctioneer held up a Medal of Honor memory coin that John Baker had donated and sent in to sell as he was unable to attend. Bob Hartman from Centreville, Va bought it for something over $300.00. He took the prize, got up and walked to Sue and my table with the auction still going on. He put out his hand and I shook it. He left that coin in my hand with tears in his eyes. I whispered "What?" He said to me, "For writing our story". He caused me to cry. I now treasure that piece for several reasons!

Some of these stories I will re-tell what the guys have told me in my words, but many of these stories I am using their words and not rewriting. Notice the different styles of writing. In most cases there will be only one event told of his tour. Every one of these guys hold hundreds of memories inside of them and most of those stories will never be shook from them.

From now on what I write will be in italics and words from other soldiers will not be.

Jerry McKinney, Oahu Hawaii: The Soldier's Friend

Jerry McKinney on a search and destroy mission Long Bien, Vietnam

Sergeant Major Jerry McKinney, stands among my most admired men I have ever had the pleasure of knowing. Generous to a fault, he is one of the most compassionate men I've ever known and a good friend, but that's not why I look up to him so much. He also had a brilliant career in the US Army and that's not why either. See, I've made many friends traveling through life and many were compassionate, some were lifer military. I admire all of those men and women. But, this is why I admire Jerry so much. I've never known a man so dedicated to a former unit as Jerry has been. Jerry was a Wolfhound, Vietnam in '67 and '68 like hundreds of other soldiers and went on to enjoy a very successful life just like so many others. After retirement in Hawaii, of course near Schofield Barracks on the island of Oahu, Jerry became very involved with the present day Wolfhounds stationed there. Mentoring and working with these young soldiers became a full time job for Jerry. Give, give and give some more to these young heroes became Jerry's life now. After he no longer worked for the Army, his daily trek to his Wolfhounds became almost a duty he could not abandon.

So amazing was this man's devotion that the Pentagon announced in 2007 that they were bestowing the title of Honorary Sergeant Major on him. Ever since the war in Afghanistan started as the planes would ready to leave Hawaii taking his beloved Wolfhounds into harms way, there is Jerry shaking hands and hugging each one as they board. As a Battalion of them come back "home" to Schofield after their tour, Now in Iraq and Afghanistan, always there is Jerry waiting, arms wide and yes, crying. Always ready with the big welcome home party all planned out and perfect. As the other Battalion leaves for the Middle East, always a send off planned and executed with great detail like one of his military operations of long ago. Standing 6 foot 4 and looking like he could run all day with a full field pack, he never tires of working for and with these heroes of today's war, our Wolfhounds of now. Jerry's Wolfhounds!

In Jerry's Words

As I was watching the History channel, there was a Program called "Shoot Out" airing. I had watched others before and saw a couple of Items about the 1st Battalion Wolfhounds in Haweiga, so I thought I would check this one out!

Damn big Mistake, It was about the TET Offensive in 1968. Needless to say, it opened up a lot of closed doors that I had kept shut for a long time. The opening part of the documentary was initially talking about D. Troop, 3d Squadron, 4th Cav.

The Aero Rifle platoon (Recon Unit) had been alerted to increased Enemy activity in the Hoc Mon Bridge Area. They were flown in to the area and shortly after, became engaged with a much superior Enemy Force. General Fred Weyand had been keeping up with the situation, two Companies from the 2nd Battalion, 27th Infantry (Wolfhounds) were airlifted into the area to pull out the Cav unit and secure the Bridge at Hoc Mon. This was the large bridge between Cu Chi and Saigon, and initial reports were that the VC/NVA were going to blow the Bridge, to prevent reinforcements from coming down from Cu Chi.

The 2 Companies (Alpha and Charlie) instantly engaged an Unknown size enemy force, aided by Helicopter Gun Ships and Artillery, they worked the Area over and secured the Hoc Mon Bridge. At the time this was happening, General Weyand requested support of two Platoons from the Wolfhounds, one would go to secure General Westmorland's Residence (Bravo Company) while the other (Delta Company) would be Airlifted to Tan Son Nhut (S) to help in Securing the Airfield.

Needless to say, all the news reporters were saying that they had no knowledge of anything going on, until the U.S. Embassy was hit that Night. We secured TSN after a brief encounter with VC/NVA and began our sweep of the Area. Suddenly a jeep pulled up, wanting to know who we were and if we knew that there was a war going on. I guess the Air force commander was running scared, and was looking to find out anything he could. We told him who we were and with the dead enemy lying in the area, we did know that there was a War going on.

After the big battle the next morning, Over 400 NVA were killed between us and the 3/4 Cav. When we finally made it back to Cu Chi, The Air force had sent 3 or 4 cases of Shot bottles, and a little over $200 for us.

And the Rest is History.

Jerry D. Mckinney
1st Platoon, Delta Company
2nd Bn, 27th Infantry
"The WOLFHOUNDS"

The shadows of the mind will always be there to accompany us on our journey thru life. This shadow is always a constant reminder of who you are, and of the "ones who stood beside you in these darkest hours."

I Love my Shadows, for they alone know how I feel.

Jerry

The Shadow

by Mariam Brooks

For all those struggling with a war that will not end.
It follows me everywhere I go
Blistering heat, driving snow
It forever changed who I am
The stench of a jungle in Viet Nam
When I close my eyes at night
I'm again embroiled in the fight
Helicopter blades chop the air and bullets fly
Wondering if I'll be the next to die
Fallen friends on the ground
Screams and crying all around
Praying and cursing in the same breath
I'm a living survivor who still feels death
Sitting up in my bed, sheets soaking wet
So many things I can't forget
I came home with a purple heart
But that my friend was just the start
The war still goes on in my mind
Friends and buddies left behind
Scars so deep they'll never heal
To me they are all too real
I'm more than just a story read
I made it home, but I'm part dead
Do not try to simplify
I can't explain it if I try
I wish I could have returned whole and sound
But part of me was left there on the ground
So I'll try my best, but don't be surprised
If you hear a scream when I close my eyes.
You weren't there, so you can't know
Nam's got control of my head and won't let go.

"Puff the Magic Dragon"

While in an exchange of thoughts, the conversation came around to "Puff the Magic Dragon." "Puff" was a fixed wing plane with mini guns sticking out the side. When they fired it in support of friendly troops the sound was a solid roar. This is Jerry McKinney's short description of that awesome machine.

Puff was great. August 1968 he was called in when Paul Lambers was fighting all night. The stream of fire he put out was a sight to behold. Paul won the Medal of Honor that night. When we got to him the next morning, there wasn't a leaf in the area that didn't have 3 or 4 holes in it.

I received this short letter from Chuck Dean (His story is later in this book) Here he talks about the "Puff" and mentions the reunion in Colorado Springs, 2011.

Don,

After reading your book, given to me from the auction in the Springs last Aug, I know another dragon. The dragon I had lived with for 45 years was a dragon that scared the hell out of me, and that fear lives with me today. We were out on a mission, and I don't remember where, but the Dragon ships were called to support us. We were pretty much in the thick of the sh** with Charlie, and the decision was made to call in "Puff". I had never heard of "Puff the Magic Dragon," other than the song. When that plane flew over the drone sounded familiar, I was familiar with the C47, or DC3, and had always been secure with the sound of the radial engines. When that thing cut loose with the mini guns, I will never forget the fear that grabbed a hold of me. Where I work we have a machine that while it is winding up I am warned that the pitch that is about to come is the same as those mini guns, only not as intense, and I can visualize 6 ropes descending from the sky raining death on whatever is in its path.

Not a 'Hound story, just a comment brother to brother.

NO FEAR Brother. Heal fast and strong

Chuck Dean

Frank Gollub

I'll let Frank tell his short story.

I went on the Sultan (troop ship) to Korea Feb 65, sailed form Oakland, Ca & got seasick, stopped in Hawaii & Yokohoma, Japan where we all got shore leave for a few hours. We sailed on to Inchon, Korea & we got on LSTs & on the way sailing in we passed a small Korean fishing boat & they gave us the finger. At Inchon we were trucked to a train & transported to the replacement center & then on to the First Cavalry near the DMZ in Korea.

I went to Vietnam from Hawaii in Jan 66 on the USS General Walker & didn't get seasick. On the way one soldier stabbed another soldier to death & the military confiscated all personal knives. We sailed on to Cam Rahn Bay where the 35th Infantry was dropped off. I remember that some kinds of explosives were dropped over the sides of the ship at night to ward off any enemy sappers. We sailed on to Vung Tau and boarded LSTs to bring us ashore. We were greeted by General Westmoreland, a band & Vietnamese Women dressed in traditional dress and they placed flower leis around our necks. We were trucked to an airfield and flown to Bien Hoa, then trucked to a staging area for a couple of weeks. We convoyed to Cu Chi and on the way I remember seeing a VC hanging from a tree and spider webs with spiders in them on the telephone wires. At Cu Chi we took over positions from the First Infantry Division and the rest is History for the Wolfhounds.

Valentine's Day is always a sad reminder to me of Valentine's Day 14 Feb 1966. The Battle for Cu Chi raged on. F O Trojan Charlie 43 Sgt Hayes & RTO PFC Morgan Starkey, an American Indian were on a sweep with 2/27 about 1000 meters in front of the perimeter when they came under heavy Viet Cong fire. Sgt George Hayes called for fire support and the Viet Cong zeroed their mortars in on them killing them both and others and wounding many men. SFC Wimp, the Weapons Platoon Sgt, asked for volunteers so Sgt "Tommie" Thompson and I volunteered to replace the FO/RTO team. May they and all the Brave Soldiers that died "Rest in Peace". God bless the wounded and God bless the living. Let us all bow our heads in prayer. Amen

William R.I. "Easy" Smith, California

Welcome Home

I arrived in Viet Nam on about the 16th of February 1967. I still recall some of those initial visions I had as I left Washington, D.C. for Oakland, California.

I remember what I was doing to this day when the letter came announcing that I had been drafted. I was working in a grocery store as the delivery boy. I went home for lunch and there it was that letter. My mother was home that day and we were going to have lunch together. Some lunch. I recall going into the bathroom and opening that letter and just before that first thump into the toilet there I was just me and that letter and this awful feeling. And I recall yelling as loud as I could to my mother "I've been drafted!"

And on August 24, 1966 I was on a bus headed for Ft. Bragg, N. C. for Basic Training. Eight weeks later I was en-route to Ft. Jackson, S.C. for AIT. What followed has become a nightmare for many veterans of the Viet Nam War.

Valentine's Day 1967 carries memories for me in that Lonnie Upchurch and I took off February 15, 1967 for Vietnam. Landed at Ton Son Nut on the 17th and on the 23rd I was in Cu Chi and a Wolfhound!

Shortly after arriving in Nam and no longer burning shit (a standard introduction to Nam for some). I gather I was considered ready for battle and sent to Chu Chi and assigned to Co A 1st Bn 27th Inf 25th Div 2nd Platoon. I don't recall getting a list of rules. I don't recall being told anymore how to survive than I had been told back in the states. I do recall and still do not understand never being in a war zone before filling up with this balance of instant fear and an instinct for survival that is difficult to explain.

I burned some more shit and washed some more dishes and before long I was no longer just I. “We” began to have more meaning in my life than ever before as we became the guy standing next to me; we became the squad; the platoon; we became the WOLFHOUNDS-THE TROPICAL LIGHTNING!

Though our stories began before we ever met, each of us from different places on the map, though we became we somewhere back in the recruiting station; or maybe it was basic training; maybe it was AIT or on the flight over or when we woke and found out that depending on each other was a new reality.

For me that fear and survival instinct melted into another reality.....would I live or would I die! The sound of friendly and enemy fire was totally different from the ghetto sounds of bullets fired by the local law enforcement chasing the bad guy; it was totally different than the sounds of fireworks on the 4th of July; no longer was the sound of bullets noise coming out of the television nor was it the sounds heard when we played cowboys and Indians and made sounds with from our mouths to imitate gunfire. THIS WAS REAL!

There seems to be no one way to tell the whole story. To see the "total impact" of the big picture. To know the truth you need only look around you. You need to take a second peek at the man or the woman or the child standing next to you. Look at the memorials, the books, the movies, the merchandise being but a fragment of what happened and you still or shall I say we find the question still remains, "Why?"

Which brings us to a new reality which immediately found tools for survival. A host of feelings that many got to experience and know about and understand them as these feelings were made present in their lives began the task of burrowing deeper and deeper into the depths of my inner self until it was as if they were no more. Feelings as we know them today, just stopped! Well, not completely. I was allowed feelings of anger. I was allowed feelings of fear. I was even allowed feelings of sadness. Oh yes, and a great deal of false bravery. But, no kiddy stuff!!!

All this and I still was not called "man". I was still a taste away from what was to be my manhood. And as I look back I still see those faces of the guys being sworn in in the recruiting station. Some looking for a back door to escape. See, the reality of going to war was still somewhat of a fantasy. The men were about to be separated from the boys.

I still see the faces of the guy on the buses. I remember the look in their eyes. That look of disassociation. That look of farewell and goodbye. One could almost picture the image of the loved ones standing in front of them waving, waving, waving for the last time.

I still see the faces as we entered deeper and deeper into the reality of war. I still recall the war games coming to an end as we got closer to the reality of war. I still recall the day we entered the reality of war.

Remember, there was a time when it may have been easier to disclose the experience of war. But, one by one the returning Viet Nam veteran met obstacles of misconceptions and rejections from society that all we could do to withstand yet another reality was to shut down, and in many cases give ourselves up to alcohol and drugs to forget!

See, society wanted to hear, but didn't want to hear. After all, the place we returned to was "fully" understanding of what we had been through, fully understanding of what we were like, fully understanding of the what it was like for us in Viet Nam to the point of not just understanding .....but knowing our deepest darkest feelings. Feelings I took even deeper within 2 days after returning to the states. Feelings that have been buried for 30 years plus. Feelings...hell, I forgot how to feel.

How did society understand the Viet Nam Veteran? How is it that the question still remains after all this time, "Why?"

The moment of truth and new realities became clear once I got my orders to go to Nam. I remember that long bus ride after AIT back to Washington, DC... Where I would have to face family, friends and America for what might be the last time. In all my newly acquired fears, not being able to tell exactly how I felt about going to war stood out the most.

People protested. There were marches. Demonstrations. Draft dodging. All kinds of feelings being expressed and acted out against the war in Viet Nam. My family never really let me know all their real feelings either. I know today somewhat why that was. I know today the fears they experienced associated with my going to Nam. I know today, that it was truly hard for them to talk to me about it. I know today the role love played in not persisting that I talk about it. It was probably the thing that made it harder for me to say goodbye. None of us knew exactly what to say. So my family did what I did in reality, they shut down and hid their feelings too! But, I saw past some of those walls just as they saw past the wall I built around me.

As for the rest of those in my surroundings. There were cries of celebration for the soldier. There were the cries of encouragement and inspiration at the bottom of every glass at the bar. It too, was a sad goodbye. Still, they celebrated my going to war. Why?

I hooked up with a friend, Lonnie Upchurch those last days in D.C. We had orders to report to Oakland in 30 days. It was the beginning of the longest goodbye ever in my life. Yet it became easier, since I didn't have to do the D.C. thing alone. The D.C. thing being a period of drinking like I had never drank before. A period of finding myself at times alone with just me and a bottle and some music. Feeling nothing. Absolutely nothing.

I thought of fleeing to Canada. Then I thought with my luck, I'd be the first one they caught. Once committing a crime came into play. But, most of the time I was too drunk or lost in the feelings of going to war that all I could deal with was living or dying.

Our 30 days got extended. Well, we overextended financially. We were late. But, knowing that we were late became somewhat of a joke. I recall once riding around the streets of D.C. and we were pulled over by the cops. Before we could pull out license and registration we informed them that we were going to Nam. We further informed them that we didn't know if we were coming back. And somehow they understood and let us go. There were other times when this new line we found "we're going to Nam and we don't know if we're coming back" worked. Hell, it worked every time we were stopped. It also became an excuse to get lost in myself and the bottle.

However, we knew eventually that we would have to go. Only problem was that we were out of money. As I recall, my brother worked at Fort Myer, Virginia (he was in the reserves then). He went to his warrant officer and got us some new orders cut and some new money. No longer could we elude the fact that we were going to Oakland. See, going to Nam hadn't fully set in yet. Well, for me, I still had not fully accepted the truth, but I was on my way.

I remember arriving in Oakland and my first shock was the weather. I arrived dressed in short sleeves and it was cold in California that day. Once we finished our little stay in Oakland we were on a TWA flight to hell. I had left behind all that felt good in life... even being alive!

I was not flattered by being given a M-16 with real bullets. I was not amused by the fumes in the air from all the shit burning; rockets and bombs; and a feeling in the air of death surrounding us on all sides. And the horror of war was there all around us.

The time had come. The introduction to Nam was over. They prepared us for war. I was in the war. And I became what I had to become to survive. No attitude adjustment was necessary.

This was real!

I still don't know "Why?"

I do know I was in Viet Nam!

The last firefight I was in in Viet Nam was on September 4, 1967, at approximately 1730 hours while on a search and destroy mission near Tay Ninh.

I don't recall how long we had been out. But, we were approaching an open field when we were ambushed by Charlie as soon as we left the tree line into an open field. We were in another firefight with an enemy barely visible.

You gotta remember, Charlie could hide his small frame of a body behind a bush or a tree, pop off a few rounds at a time and pin down a whole platoon for days. This was done while he puffed on a cigar or a joint and ate handfuls of rice and raw chicken.

On this day he hit 2 of our men. It could have been more, which was difficult for me to tell. All I know is that there was heavy fire being laid out in front of us and the gun ships and artillery didn't make it any easier to comprehend the entire situation.

What I do know is that these 2 men who were hit were in my squad. I think one was Sgt. Joe Riley (still not good on complete names) my friend. I knew I had to do something.

The way I remember it was I looked at the man next to me and yelled, "gotta get my friend!!!!" and took off to the open field. I don't remember if I took my weapon with me, I doubt it since it was a M-60 caliber machine gun.

I took off keeping low as possible. I was able to pull the first man back to the tree line to await medical evacuation. I don't recall who I pulled back first. I got back to the open field and put the second man across my shoulder and headed for the tree line. I didn't get far before I felt myself releasing him.

As I released the man I was carrying and not by choice, I got this awful feeling in the pit of my stomach. I fell. I don't recall making a sound at that moment. I stared into the heaven above. I could hear and feel the gun fire and rockets all around me from the firefight that was taking place. I couldn't see the man I was carrying just seconds before. I felt like lying there had been forever. I was overcome by this empty feeling over my entire body.

As I lay there I could see visions of loved one---my mother--my daughter and my then wife. I was - I was - I was immobile. I was hit. I took a round from a rocket. I couldn't feel anything in my legs. I didn't know if I was alive or dead. A scare set in. A fear set in. I was angry. I was worried about everyone else. I was out of the battle.

I had been wounded before. And I returned to the battle. But, this time I couldn't return to help my comrades. I had this feeling I had let them down by getting hit. I wanted to be with them. It was not like in the movies when a buddy walks over to you as you lay on the stretcher and says "hey may, you're going home!" Instead one of the guys said they're going to give you a Silver Star. I never saw him again. This was not the movies. And I encountered a feeling of guilt. I had learned to fight. I had become a warrior. And I didn't feel like a hero. I was doing my job!!!!

The picture is vague of the chopper lift off. It took so long to get there as it was difficult to land because the LZ (landing zone) was hot. It felt like forever and I left the field that day without being able to say, "Goodbye!"

William "Easy" Smith has written many Essays and is a prolific poet. I asked him which of his many poems was his favorite. I give you:

VIETNAM WARRIOR: ANOTHER DREAM/ANOTHER REALITY

Thought I was a cowboy
cap pistoling away

Liked to be the cop too
til I lost my toy gun one day

When I played the bad guy
being the ganster didn't pay
my parents didn't go for that
in my room I had to stay

Climbed up on my wooden horse
clinching it's mopped hair

Found out I was dreaming
to miss childhood isn't fair

I was told to get some schooling
comes in handy and that's no fooling

Played spin the bottle
and doctor and nurse
even played mom and dad
but wasn't allowed to curse

Found out I was dreaming
reality set in how sad

Watched all the Tarzan movies
but he didn't have a gun

Yet with all his courage

King of the jungle seemed like fun

Saw all the war movies
thought soldiering would be fine

I knew they would be calling me
it was just a matter of time

Started thinking about what my father said
stories of comrades he no longer saw

He told me of his journey
in another war

And those he would not see again
the reason they were dead

They died so that we may live
these warriors of the past

For freedom is what he said
For our freedom they bled

I thought I had the edge on things
As I heard about the war in Southeast Asia

New feelings entered my head
more thinking about the things my daddy said

Started remembering my childhood heroes
figured I'd do just fine

But soon I was in the war
and reality changed my mind

I mustered up some courage

and renewed my faith in God

Didn't know if it would help or not
as I realized no more were the games

I was in a place called Vietnam
with all faces and new names

Some were known by general
we had Sergeants and Privates too
Tunnel rats and radio men
just to name a few

Some units were called companies
broken down four squads made a platoon
We travelled with a medic
He took care of the wounds

I saw in this new life
as a renewed temporary stay on earth

Thought many times I'd get it
and never again see my place of birth

I had me a real gun
shooting bullets was no fun

Especially when being shot at
by an enemy always on the run

But there I was where I became a man
the day my life as a combat warrior
had only just begun

Under skies filled with the burning of human waste
and the stench of lifeless blood

We fought in rubber plantations
and rice paddies turned to mud

Where rockets landed in the rainy season
fighting not knowing the reason

I saw my buddies leave the wire
not everyone returned
Changed my belief in God

The bombs the fell without pity
as we fought in unknown cities

Sometimes in heavy battles
we suffered great loss

But we forged on
peace and freedom was our boss

Finally found a reason
renewed my faith in God

Travelled through mine filled roads
and slept in two man foxholes

Some days we missed a meal
part of the unwritten deal

Now and then we got to laugh
most times we were on alert
just one mistake easy to get hurt

Each man became a link
in a combat chain
fighting for freedom and democracy

so call us by our names

Though when the war was done
and we returned to where we'd begun

No welcome mat was laid
we had no warriors' parade

But we were not discouraged
at least not by all the things we saw

We had fought for our country
in a foreign war

We left the embraces of family charms
we set aside our dreams

We answered to our country's
To Arms To Arms To Arms

We did our job
and there's honor in that
renewed my faith in God

Call us what you like
say about us what you feel
remember where we've been
it's not fiction it was real

We are combat Veterans

Easy.

Larry "Deacon" Brown

Left to right: Larry Campbell, Bill Franklin, Deacon Brown

I must include this long tall Texan in this book as well. Simply because he was one of the most amazing of my brothers. He was, and is today, one of the most solid, everyday followers of Jesus that I know. He never wavered. I think most of our unit was Christian men and of course we all stumbled, Christian speaking, with language and other things. But never the Deacon. Everyone was Deacon's friend and I found no faults in him. If one man in my past had anything to do with my strength of faith even today, it has to be him. Vietnam would test a man's faith with just the pure terror of it all. The weather, insects, death all around and the uncertainty of the future all wore a man down spiritually. None of it shook the Deacon's faith however.

He got a nick name quickly like most of the guys. A nick name usually came within the first minute of meeting with your group or anytime later. Larry would always take advantage of the make do Church services in the field when the Chaplain came around. Those services were usually in the open with the men sitting on their knees and the Chaplain giving a five minute sermon. Larry Brown would ask guys to come with him to the service and a turn down wasn't recommended with him. He was about 6 ft 4 and tough as nails, so when he grabbed your shirt and pulled, you went along peaceably! One day one of the guys going through that ritual asked Larry if he was "some sort of a Deacon or what?" That was it. From then on he was the Deacon.

I am honored to be asked to speak several times a year and the most enjoyable for me is when I get to address young people either in high school or Church youth groups. I always manage to get "Deacon" Brown stories squeezed in the speech to youth. Young folks are pressed by peer pressure so hard now and doing as the others is so important to them because they need to "fit" in. When I use the Deacon stories, I explain that even when Christian kids are made fun of and called stupid names, when times gets black, those that made the fun will always lean on the Christian.

It was clear where the true strength was when things were the blackest. Everyone loved the Deacon.

A short note from "our" Deacon:

It says in the Bible to call no man a fool. However, it does not say that I cannot call myself a fool.

You see, before I was drafted, my job was in management. So, after basic training and leave, I was to report back to find a great job for me! I was so smart when I walked in the class and everyone was typing, I thought I would die on the spot. You see, I didn't know how to type, because back in the early '60's, boys didn't type in my school unless you wanted to be called a sissy.

I told the instructor that I would do anything to get out of typing. Now you know where the "I can call myself a fool" comes in. Has anyone heard about the foot soldier? Yes, I could have been typing, but instead I was assigned to the Infantry.

My second bright idea was to sign up for Hawaii. Was I a fool? The buddies in Basic told me, "Only enlisted men go to Hawaii. You were drafted!" Well, I showed them! After AIT, I was on a ship to paradise, to Hawaii! I couldn't figure out why I needed special boots in Hawaii. But, I was there only three months when I shipped out again, this time on a slow boat to....yes, Viet Nam. I could have been typing!

All 5000 of us had these special boots for this special trip. But, I didn't want to be typing, did I?

I wouldn't take anything for my boots and buddies in the 27th Infantry Wolfhounds! And, I won't call myself a fool for my experiences and my memories.

Private Larry "Deacon" Brown

Leonard "Ski" Slizoski: Race Driver

Leonard "Ski" Slizoski and me. 1966 Cu Chi Vietnam

Ski was one of the best buddies I ever had. There were about six of us guys hung together most of the time in Hawaii and Ski was one of that bunch. We saw many funny things together but I must tell of one ordeal we were in just him and me. It was not long after the 25th Division had finally settled on the Cu Chi area in Vietnam to build a base camp. It was still very brushy and had much timber standing (jungle actually).

The Regiment and Division had a lot of "mini" CP's (Command Posts) scattered around the circumference of our new camp. Ski and I were digging our squad size hole and filling sandbags as we were told to do when an officer came up to us (not ours) and asked if one of us could drive a jeep. I said not a word of course, but Ski answered, "Sure sir," and we were immediately taken away from our unit. Officer guy pointed to me and said "shotgun" and told Ski he was driver. We were to drive these narrow paths from one CP to another carrying some sort of vital information (sure it was).

For several days this was our job and we just wanted to be back with our buddies. Snipers were still inside the camp during this time and taking shots at the good guys quite often. We were told by officer guy to drive fairly slow, but as soon as we got a piece away from a CP, Ski wound the ol' girl up and hummin' we went. We took a round from sniper Charlie once in a while and on many of those trips we had 60 mortars drop somewhere around us. But our speedy jeep was too slippery for our slow witted enemy mortar man.

Using the same route everyday must have gave Dim Wit enough chances to get our skinny little dusty road zeroed in pretty well because on one eventful trip we had a 60 land right in the middle of the road ahead of us 25 yards. By the time Ski got jeep stopped another dropped as Ski jammed the little army car in reverse and back we went as fast as it would run with me running rounds out of my M14 as fast as it would go. Bad guy was walking rounds right down the road toward us til we got out of range. I was absolutely positive Ski was going to either wreck the thing or it would throw a rod and stall any minute.

It wasn't funny during the race, but afterwards it was like many things that went on in Vietnam, became funnier as time went on. He laughed at me for shooting at .....well, nothing and I laughed at him trying to hold a speeding jeep on a narrow dusty road going way too fast! He could no more see through the dust we had just stirred up going forward than he could fly a jet. Luck kept us between the trees.

Highest Traditions: Tony Lazzarini

Tony Lazzarini making his M60 and his "slick" ready for the work day.

I got a call from a friend of mine, an old Wolfhound by the name of William "Easy" Smith. He advised me to get in contact with a group known as "The Military Writers Society of America" because of my book. He knew an author that was involved with them and that they were a good group of about 800 authors. I guess he talked me into it, because I did and it has been a good experience.

Anyway, about 2 weeks after I sent in my info to join the group, I got this call from a guy named Tony Lazzarini. He said he was the president of MWSA and he normally didn't review books any more as he had a staff of writers handle that, but he had reviewed it. He said he wanted to do that because on the front cover I had written "Wolfhound". He knew the Wolfhounds well he said, and then he went into detail. He was based at Cu Chi the same time I was and had been in Hawaii the same as I. He did extend for six months, which turned into nine after I left however. So he did 21 months in Nam. His unit, the 25th Aviation, was the taxi service for the Wolfhounds along the other units of the 25th Division. Sort of a coincidence there. Tony was a door gunner in one of the "Little Bear" slicks (Huey). He said he was going to write a positive review on the web site about my book and for me to take a look at it.

Tony then told me I should consider bringing some books to Branson to the MWSA annual convention the first week in November and sign some books. I did drive down there and had a wonderful time. I met and made many new friends and got well acquainted with Tony Lazzarini. He was in charge of the convention so he was a pretty busy fellow.

Tony's and my dates of service mirrored so, even though we had different jobs, we had much in common. I have read one of his three books that he authored, "Highest Traditions" and I tell everyone that it is one of the best I've ever read. It is a very easy to read, non-offensive and informative book for anyone wanting to get inside of a door gunner's head for a moment. I warn you, you don't want to stay inside the head of an old Huey crewman for very long however!

The next story involves Tony or is because of him at least.

Butch Allen, Osceola, Missouri: Because of the Book

I have had several phone calls and meetings with amazing individuals as a result of the "See The Dragon" book. I have been privileged to meet many authors at signings, which led to other acquaintances that I now value greatly. None are more amazing than the following story.

I arrived in Branson, MO to attend the Veterans' reunion and also the Gathering of the Military Writers Society as their president, Tony Lazzarini, suggested I do. The second day there about mid-day I heard this crazy man yelling from down the hall "Hey Arndt, look what I've found for you." It was Tony again, only this time through he had a man with his wife following behind him. Tony tells me that he's found another Wolfhound and the guy had not seen or talked to another Hound since Nam.

So this new guy and I were introduced and then we proceeded to have a great visit. Since there were folks from all over the Nation, he asked me where I was from. I told him he wouldn't know my little town, but it was about an hour south of Kansas City. He asked again, so I said, "Adrian." He said, "Sure, I'm from Osceola!" A side note, this couple lived in Osceola, MO which is only about 1 ½ hours south of my home. They are Arthur "Butch" and Vicki Allen and it was really fun sharing with them stories of past reunions that he didn't even know were happening. He was excited to find that there was an organization and newsletters and wanted to join. I think his wife was more excited to hear about reunions than Butch was.

This is sort of a three part coincidence thing. I'll try to un-confuse it as best as I can.

The Wolfhounds have what they call a relay on the net that is used for updates and goings on within the old Hounds. When I got home from Branson, I got on this relay and asked the Secretary to send a Wolfhound newsletter to Butch (the new guy) so he could join and get started. Of course all members of the relay get the messages. Almost immediately I got a reply from Paul "Gabby" Gaither, one of the relay members. The message read like it was an emergency. Gabby wrote that he had been trying to find this guy Allen for nearly 40 years. He said that in Nam, Arthur's nick name was "Coyote". They were best friends in Nam and he needed Arthur's phone number if I had gotten it at Branson from him. I sent the number right back to him. That evening I talked to Butch (or Coyote) on the phone and he told me that Paul had called him and they were making plans to "hook up" very soon. Paul lives in North Carolina so it will be quite a drive for them, but I knew it would be a real site to witness that reunion.

I did get to witness that. Gabby and Coyote had both agreed to hook up at the Branson reunion in 2010 and I was there to see it. There is nothing quite like watching two best friends see each other for the first time in over 40 years.

Boy, the people you meet

While I was stationed at my desk at the Branson signing/Vet reunion, there were two men about my age stopped to visit. I figured some more vets because the place was swarming with them by then. Veterans were everywhere! They stood and talked a while then took a chair and talked some more, mostly about "old times" in the 50s. One bought my book so I asked him if he was Army or what so I would know how to sign it for him. He said neither of them had served, but were there just in support and that they had great admiration for our vets. Nice fellows for sure. After about 30 minutes they decided they needed to move on and look around and the taller of the two said to me that I should come back down some day and come see their show. Of course I asked what show. One of them said he was the sax player with Bill Haley's Comets, Joe D'Ambrrusio. The taller one then said he was Dick Richards, the drummer. They each handed me a card with their phone numbers on them and said when we got to Branson to call one of them and our tickets would be free at the Dick Clark Theater. What a deal, I had grew up listening to them. They said they were the originals and had played all these years!

Otto "Lenny" Leonard, Belaire, Ohio

Otto Leonard (left) and Don Arndt at Cu Chi base camp, March 1966

"I'll hold em, you guys get out"

Now I want to tell you about a good buddy and a decorated, honest to goodness hero. Lenny spoke fluid German and he took it upon himself to teach me as much of the language that I was able to learn.

I met Lenny in Hawaii in July 1965 and we became instant friends. I thought then that he was just like the rest of us as we trained together and we laughed together. It wouldn't be until Vietnam that I really learned what Lenny was really like. We all know people that are generous to a fault, those that would, as they say, "give you the shirt off their back." In the war I knew men that way, only there they chose to give their life for their squad buddies. Men that chose in a spilt second made a decision to offer themselves up to save others. Lenny was one of those men. This is the real Otto "Lenny" Leonard.

The Army standard pack for a M-79 grenade launcher was 20 rounds. The rounds were each very heavy, so most '79ers had other men around him become ammo bearers carrying extra rounds for them. Lenny did that too, but instead carrying one 20 round bag himself, he carried much more. Carrying his pack and so many extra M-79 rounds was extremely difficult, but it proved to be the difference for him and his unit on more than one occasion.

The particular contact with the enemy, that he had been recognized for valor is a rather lengthy story, but Lenny's version goes like this: It was April 5th, 1966. Lenny was part of a 13 man LP just north of the Company (120 men) about a click. It was about 4am when an enemy unit began to enter our small area. The LP made contact with a force of about 300 Communist soldiers. They were in three columns of 100 each. The center column was the most pressing problem. It was decided to attack that center column. Lenny's constant fire from that, now famous M-79, was inflicting heavy damage on them, along with the fire power of the rest who were all small arms equipped. However, it became evident after something over an hour that the patrol would be overrun very soon because it was so vastly outnumbered. At that time it was decided to regroup very quickly with the main body to the south. Knowing that a retreat would most surely be suicide, as the enemy was so close; Lenny and his buddy said they would stay at that position and hold them long enough for the remaining 11 men to marry up with our main force in order to form something with a little more military advantage. Knowing that no one would ever see either of them alive again, the patrol made their way back to the Company.

After the patrol had withdrawn from the position and Lenny and the other kid was alone, one enemy platoon made an attempt to overrun the two men's position, but Lenny and his M-79 repelled that assault. The Viet Cong then made a military blunder. They allowed the onslaught of Lenny's grenade launcher to split them into two units and they then attempted to flank the two of them plus the Company at the same time. At that time the Company became fully engaged and after about 30 minutes the operation turned in the favor of Company A. The enemy became disorganized and broke off the engagement.

Shortly after the fire fight had ended, Lenny came limping, no, not limping... sort of sliding one leg, into the company area carrying his friend. Lenny had a wound in his left knee and was bleeding badly. Either a bullet or chunk of shrapnel from a grenade had got him. It was amazing that he could walk, let alone able to carry a man his own size a few hundred meters out of that stench and smoke-filled valley of death.

I had a good 35 mm camera that I had bought while in Hawaii. Lenny always told me I would be shot someday just taking pictures with my camera in my hand. Lenny said he remembers that I was always yelling, "Wait a minute, I gotta get a picture of that!"

My friend Lenny passed away in 2011.

Merrill Sellers, Orangevale, California

I want you to now meet one of the most colorful men I know. This is a guy that after 10 minutes with him you think you've known him a lifetime. The single most outstanding trait I see in Merrill is his generosity and compassion toward fellow brothers of the war. (Especially Wolfhounds!) He is the all time great "finder" of buddies. Men trying desperately to locate long since lost friends from the Vietnam war are being brought together by this man because of the gift he has. They give Merrill a nickname, unit and time frame and somehow almost like magic two best friends are suddenly together! All of us are blessed by his friendship. I'll let him tell some of his story in his words:

I was born and raised in the Sacramento, California, area. At the time I got my "special letter" to report, I was working at a W.T. Grants, department store. We called them "Five 'n Dimes" in those days. That's when the eatery had a counter, and round stools to sit on. My main duty was to keep the store clean and put up fixtures for displays. I doubled as a security agent watching for petty theft High Schoolers from a nearby campus. This was my first real money making adventure.

On November 6, 1967, I was inducted into the Army in Oakland, CA. and was sent to Fort Lewis, WA to receive my basic military training, including a brand new wardrobe and special running boots. I knew this was the place to be! After the flight from Sacramento to Sea-Tac airport, I was bussed to the company area. D 5 – 2. My home to be. We arrived at the company compound late at night and went directly to the mess hall. The eggs went down on the griddle, the mess Sgt asked how we wanted them, and no matter what we requested, the eggs were all the same. The whites were still clear and the yolks bright and cheery. That was my first mess hall experience. The platoon sergeant said, "YOU AREN'T HERE TO CHEW!!! SWALLOW IT AND GET OUT!!!" I just had my first military humor experience. Even today, I chuckle when I remember those words. As an E-1 or E-2 we were taking orders from E-4s.

My Platoon Sgt was Sgt Blount, a black guy that could count cadence, and sing the marching songs like a bird. I mean, it was pretty! The whole platoon liked Sgt Blount. He was a buck Sergeant. His enforcer Staff sergeant, a short little white guy with

E-6 stripes did most of the yelling. He had just returned from his tour in Vietnam, and thought he was immortal. He was wearing a 1st Air Cav patch. Nobody remembers his name. Fort Lewis was cold in November and December, so we weren't allowed to act normal. No gloves or hands in our pockets. No standing in the coal furnace room waiting for early morning formation. We had to hold ourselves in readiness at all times in case of an emergency or something? By the end of our cycle, I was ready for another army. Next was AIT training at Fort Polk, LA. Tigerland, peace on ridge or something that sounds close to that, was the best jungle training we could get. I was ready.

After a 30 day break from Army life, I flew to vietnam. I use a small V because communist countries don't deserve Capitalist letters. Arriving at Bien Hoa airport, we were bussed to the 90th replacement center at Long Bien. Lots of good, volunteerism here for two or three days until being assigned a unit. I was lucky! Co D 1/27 25th Inf Division was my new "home away from home". After a week of intense jungle training in Cu Chi, I was flown out to the field with some other new guys, to our company location in some FSB.

George Watts was a special guy. He was also new. He was from Georgia, and would call me "Sells". "Hey Sellllls", what's goin' on? We were good buds the whole year and eventually left on the same plane back to the world. I met Cliff Summers and

Don Nichols, members of the squad that I was assigned to. My first night in the field was an eye opener. My squad went on an ambush. The ambush site was an old road leading to a village. We were told to stop by the local ARVN compound to pick up some trainees, and introduce them to the ambush experience. These guys were not only trainees, they didn't think much about fighting. They brought their portable boom boxes for the tunes, and chattered all night long. On another occasion; a company operation, we were ambushed in front of an ARVN compound; by the same military personnel we were to take with us.

Smitty was a pot smoker. Before he smoked his home made rolls, he would dip them in the perfume that he picked up from the local "ladies of the night". We called them Boom-Boom girls. I'm sure the fumes really blended well to make a special treat at the end of a long day. Smitty went nuts in the field. He left the perimeter several times, without his weapon, and spent time at the nearby village, sweet talkin' the girls. The CO sent a squad to locate him several times.

One night, he was point man on our platoon ambush patrol. We silently walked into a village, somehow managing to evade the VC guards that were placed around the perimeter. Ole' Smitty walked right into a hooch. There was a meeting going on with the local VC leaders in this hooch. I was carrying the platoon radio for Plt Sgt Williams, and was monitoring the traffic.

The next thing I knew, we saw people running around the hooches. We didn't know what was goin' on, until a VC, carrying an AK-47, ran around the corner on the hooch we were next to. He actually ran into me and turned and headed out to the wood line. Platoon Sgt Williams nailed him as he was in panic mode. Then, we heard more rounds going off on the other end of the village. We pulled back out of the village and set up our ambush in a wood line not far from the village and the main dirt road going to the village. Shortly after midnight, This lambretta comes up the road with his lights on. He stops near the area where the VC was killed and after a few minutes, he leaves the village, back the way he came in. I was on the radio with HQ and they said "Don't fire on him". We were only to observe??? Figure that one out. We had a 90 MM at our position and could have really, lit up that lambretta.

On a lighter note: We had a Killer (Arty) forward observer with us on a company sweep somewhere near the delta, with lots of rice paddies and lots of "blues" to cross. The killer RTO was a Sacramento guy named Bill Grigsby. He was a short guy, carrying a radio that was seemed to cover his whole, upper torso. Every time he tried to jump across the blue, that radio would pull him back in the water. He would then, come out of the water, using every word NOT in the dictionary in those days, and he was fit to be tied. We couldn't help but laugh at his situation. I was also carrying the radio and knew how difficult it was.

There was a two month period, when I had to hump the 90MM as well as my M16. It was a real aggravating experience. It was hard enough, walking through bamboo hedgerows and wood lines, and heavily wooded areas, with your M16 and all the junk you were carrying, and not get hung up on something. When I carried that 90MM, I had to sling my M16 around my back (which kept working its way back to my arms) and try to work the length of the 90MM through the bush. I thought that a 90MM was a weapon platoon item. I thought a 45 caliber weapon was the proper backup?? I was sure grateful for my RTO assignment. No more point, no more 90MM.

George Watts and I got off line and went to Tay Nihn for a few days and then Cu Chi before heading to out process from the unit. Tay Nihn was on full alert that week, and George and I, being Wolfhounds and 11B MOS, were placed in the main bunker at the entrance to the base camp. There was talk of a ground attack, so we were nervous and stayed awake most of the night.

About 2 AM, some rockets came slamming inside the perimeter. We were fully awake. There was a period of total silence, it seemed like five minutes. Then out of the silence, while the whole camp is listening for more activity, came this funny comment. It was a black guy somewhere on the bunker line, saying in a real, strong, slow voice, “THIS ARMY’S ALLLLLLLL RIGHT!!!!” The whole perimeter opened up with laughter. I can still hear his voice. It was a good ending for what could have been, a terrible night.

My first day in the field, with company D, 1st Wolfhounds , started in mid-afternoon, as George Watts and I, and a few other hounds, boarded the back end of a Ch-47 with our weapons and field gear. We flew to the FSB that was set up in a deserted rice patty area. The berms were still there, but the water had dried up. I remember looking out the porthole windows of the Chinook, checking out the sandbagged bunkers around the perimeter and the steel culverts that were used for protection. After off-loading the Chinook, we we're assigned to our platoon and squad. That's where I met Don Nichols (Nick) and Cliff Summers.

After a short intro to the platoon area, we were told to "saddle up" for bush. I had no idea what we were getting into. After walking a short distance we were hooked up with some ARVN's that were not real committed to the program. We walked until we reached our ambush location. As we were grouped in two or three man positions along a small river, we hoped for a quiet, un-eventful night of zero contact with Charlie. Instead, we were soon to be in a confrontation with the "goofy" ARVNs and their radios blasting away. Everybody in the world knew we were there! The rest of the night was uneventful, and walking back into the perimeter in the morning was a relief for me. Just in time for some chow and a perimeter bunker assignment. We later had another joint ARVN ambush experience. As we were walking down the dirt road leading to their compound, someone "opened up" on our point element. It must have been the same bunch that we met before!

My friend, George Watts, was too cool to be in the army. He had a southern Georgia way of missing half the letters in my name. My name was Sellers - George would say - "Hey Saaales" what's happ'nin'. I always got a kick out of it and after all these years, I can still hear him in my mind. He always wore his steel pot backwards (like many of us did). When he walked point, he was just as slow. He must have had something besides "war" on his mind. We all liked him. I located his family eight years ago in a small country town in Georgia. George had passed away 5 years before, and his wife was happy with the fact that "George had found the Lord" and was saved. Amen. I hope to see him again someday.

"Curly" Boyles was from the San Francisco Bay area. He was probably the best point man in the platoon. He also wore his steel pot backwards -- maybe a rebellious streak from the peace crowd. He did like his moments of cannabis and base camp refreshment. He was a best buddy of Larry Malone. I think they both came in on the buddy draft system. They were both from the Bay area.

Larry told me a few years ago about the time Curly quit the war! The FSB was doing their routine free fire around the perimeter, and someone opened up with a M-60 from a position that was above the bunker assigned to Curly. He was sooo mad, and upset, mainly because he was real short (ready to go home), that he grabbed his weapon and stomped all the way over to the company commanders hooch and let himself in. He said, "I QUIT". The Company Commander gave him something else to do until Deros date. When Larry told me the story he couldn't stop laughing. I think he was high.

Donald Dale, Clovis, New Mexico: Texas Boy

I met Donald during mid 1965. Donald Dale and I arrived in Hawaii near the same time and were both assigned to Schofield Barracks. That's where we both joined the 27th Infantry Regiment though we were separated into different jobs. He remained in the truck driver business as well he should have because that was the school he had just graduated from in Fort Leonard Wood in Missouri. I, on the other hand, was captured by the Commo platoon Sgt. The Commo platoon Sgt began the process of changing my MOS from truck driver to "Field Wireman". I had not a clue what the job entailed, but I was to learn by OJT, which I attempted to do.

Back to Donald Dale. Donald and I were great friends, him being an old farm boy too, only he was from Texas. Seems like the rural boys grouped together pretty often. Sort of birds of a feather kind of thing. We went to Vietnam together on the troop ship and he remained a Wolfhound the entire tour.

In 2008, Sue and I traveled to Salt Lake City to attend a Wolfhound reunion. After the reunion, we came home the southern route through Arizona and New Mexico with the intention of stopping for a time so I could visit my old friend now living in Clovis, NM.

He had been a Texas farm boy, so after his military service, he returned there to spend his life doing what he loved, farming. He married Nita in 1969 and they had two daughters. A few years ago Donald contacted Parkinson's disease so the farm was sold and he and Nita moved across the line to Clovis where they spend the next few years of their retirement. A very Spiritual man, Don was for years a Deacon in their Baptist Church.

So, Sue and I arrived in Clovis and found their home, but it would not be a quick hi and good bye. We stayed the night, took meals together and had a great time the next day "catching up" after 42 years. He was the same as when I knew him. Oh sure, his body was broken, he couldn't walk without assistance, he had much trouble with most functions, but Donald was still the same inside. Same heart and same humor as I once knew. I was walking with him outside as he shuffled along very slowly, stopping often, and then moving again with his walker. I said, Don, you don't move as fast as when I knew you last. He replied, "Well Don, I only have two speeds now, I've got this one and then one that's real slow."

A year after I saw him, he had to start living in the local nursing home as Nita just couldn't handle the big, gentle man any longer. He was just too big a guy for her to lift up out of the bed and chairs. I am so glad I was blessed with the opportunity to see him and meet his wonderful wife.

Since we didn't work together in Vietnam and our paths only crossed briefly from time to time, we each had many stories to share. We laughed with each other when we told the tales of great humor.

Of course his stories were the things he got into and saw while driving his deuce and a half running supplies and ammo to and fro. He said many times they traveled with tanks mixed in the column. One day he saw a 1964 Pontiac GTO sitting on the road with no one around. He couldn't believe it, a 64 GTO! There wasn't enough room on the narrow road for the tank to go around and so the M48 ran over the front of that beautiful car mashing it to the ground. The convoy never stopped or even slowed down.

We traded a few tales of "close calls" of course. He said on one of those trips the tank he was immediately following ran over an anti tank mine and it blew the track off of it stopping it dead. That was the beginning of an ambush. There was a short fire fight following, but the good guys made short work of it.

I'll interrupt the men's stories to tell some reunion tales.

The 2007 Wolfhound Reunion in Lexington, KY

See The Dragon was published just before the reunion in Lexington, KY had taken place. I was very excited about that upcoming event and it turned out to be more than I had hoped for. This is "The rest of the story", sort of the next chapter of my first book.

Sue and I left for the reunion a couple of days early to spend a day and night with the Shea's at their invitation. They were indeed going to the reunion, but would meet up with us three days later. They live outside of Junction, IL on a large farm. One of the chapters in my book is titled, "John Shea and basic training".

One thing I soon learned is that there were more than just the two of us that trained in Ft Leonard Wood Missouri and was stationed together in Hawaii together than just John and I. I had forgotten about Dennis Burger. I wish I hadn't because he is a great guy. We just weren't together in Hawaii at all and I had forgotten about him. Also he was not allowed to ship to Vietnam with the rest of us due to an allergic reaction to some of the shots required. He remained in Hawaii during the war. Anyway, I learned that Dennis only lived a rocks throw from John and Alene's farm, so John and I drove over for a great visit then Dennis came over and had meal with us at the Shea's home. We had such a good time. John and Alene have had a wonderful life and own a beautiful farm in southern Illinois. John and I looked over his place and had long visits. The next morning Sue and I loaded up and continued our trek to Lexington.

It is so rewarding to me to have proof that those heroes I had known, worked with and loved were really the great guys I thought they were at the time instead of only thinking so and they not really being men of such fiber. It becomes more evident to me at each meeting that I was indeed privileged to be around men such as these. Every one of them I find and "hook up" with after all these decades are amazing men with fine values and all are possessing enormous drive to excel. Just good men, everyone.

This time in Lexington turned out to be the best reunion ever and not really because the attendance had grown in numbers again, but for the shear numbers of special meetings and reunions that happened within the reunion.

As soon as we arrived and checked in, we started meeting old friends from reunions in the past and the hugs started. John and Sherry Babbitt were our first hugs and he immediately said "where's the books?" I told him they were in the truck in the parking lot, so I made a run (OK, I walked slow with a limp) to get a few of them. I had taken about 60 or 70 at John's request. He had assured me that no one would take it as me taking advantage of the meeting just to hawk books. The wolfhounds in attendance bought nearly all my books and by the third day I was getting reviews back from them reading it. They made me feel so good with their positive comments.

John Babbitt, Dave Hunt and Merrill Sellers had a mini reunion with the mother and sister of one of their friends that had gotten killed in Nam.

I had hoped that a least 6 of the men I had wrote about, my friends/brothers would be there, but there were only three of us. Bill Franklin called me and said they had to cancel at the last moment because he was taking his wife to the hospital. (She is fine now) Still that was a big deal. Deacon Brown, John Shea and I, all with our wives met and anticipated the arrival of Charlie Crowe's sister and her husband. The next day they arrived and we greeted Charlie Crowe's sister, Patsy Clayton. She and her husband, Earl, had driven to the reunion to meet the close friends of her brothers. Much crying of joy as we all hugged, but that was not the end of it. The word spread throughout ranks of the 140 Wolfhounds and they all wanted to express their love for Charlie even though they didn't know him. Charlie was their brother too. I asked Patsy how many hugs she had got and she said she had lost count.

A few weeks after the reunion, I spoke to Patsy. She told me how much she and Earl enjoyed the meeting and tried to explain what a healing time it was for her to visit with Charlie's friends.

The Banquet, Two Very Special Moments

Friday evening was the Wolfhound banquet and I believe all that attended the reunion were there. The mini reunions all sat together at their own tables just as at our table sat Sue and I, John and Alene Shea, Deacon and Diane Brown and Earl and Patsy Clayton. At one table sat John and Sherry Babbitt, Merril and Rebeca Sellers and Dave and Brenda Hunt.

After the meal they started the annual auction held to keep a treasury for reunions, scholarships and such. The President of our Association, Gary Huber, became the auctioneer and the first thing he held up was a See the Dragon book. He said "Well you all know what this is. It is the book that was donated and passed around for every one of you Wolfhounds to sign," So this book brought a lot of money. I didn't know who bought it.

One of the most memorable moments of the 6 day event was when they held up an 18 inch long shinny black replica of the Vietnam Wall. It was bringing a lot of money and Larry Deacon Brown, sitting at our table, was bidding every other time. The bidding was finally over and Deacon had bought the "Wall" for many times what it was worth. Deacon walked up and paid, took it from Gary and returned to our table. But instead of sitting down, he first walked to Charlie Crowe's sister Patsy and handed the memento it to her. That was very emotional for every one who witnessed it.

After the evening was over and everyone was done with the group photos, I worked my way toward the hall to go to my room. I heard someone yell for me and it was Dave Hunt. I went over and he held up a Dragon book and said this is yours. I told him that it wasn't mine cause I was out of books. He insisted and handed it to me. When I looked at it, it was the one that all the Wolfhounds had signed. Dave was the one that had bought it at Auction and he told me that it was my book, and then all those around him said that no one should have it but me. I couldn't believe it. I had a death grip on it as I said that I couldn't accept it. I read every name in it after I got to my room. They were all there. I read one signature that said "Charlie Crowe, by Sister Patsy Clayton" Wow! That was big. Then I saw that General Robert Foley had signed it "Robert Foley". Not Medal of Honor winner Robert Foley, not General Robert Foley... no, just his name. He was a Capt and company Commander in November of 1966 during an operation where his company was attempting to rescue another company that was in deep trouble. His actions and the actions of Sgt Baker earned them both the M.O.H. What amazing men!

So, I have that book in my office with my most prized possessions. Certainly not because it is a "See the Dragon" book, but because it has over 100 heroes, brothers, and friends signatures in it.

There Was a Very Sad Time, Too

There were two 12th Evac nurses attended the Lexington reunion. They served at the Cu Chi base camp at the MASH unit during Vietnam. I thought it was great that they were with us in Lexington. They were bubbly and laughing and crying with all the emotions one would expect.

Ann Cunningham was one of the two Nurses and of course I had to have a turn at hugging her and thanking her for her sacrifice. She was at the hospitality room with all of the Wolfhounds and of course attended the Wolfhound banquet on Friday evening. Saturday she was running around visiting and having a great time. At the 25th Division banquet Saturday evening she didn't attend. Like everyone else, I wondered why she wasn't there.

Sue and I left Lexington and headed home to Missouri at 4:30 the next morning. We didn't know until we got home and looked on the relay that she had had a stroke and died just before the banquet Saturday evening. Such a great lady. In Hawaii during the 25th Division's reunion in 2006, she had given me a hat pin depicting the nurse's monument in DC that stands close the Vietnam Wall. I keep it on my VFW hat and think of her sacrifice every time I see it.

More Stories

Tom Donovan, Oxford, Ohio: Light Contact

In 2008, when Sue and I got home from our 3 ½ week trip that included a four day meeting with my Wolfhounds, I saw that I had a boat load of messages on my machine. One of those was a two week old message from a man by the name of Tom Donovan stating that he had just finished reading the Dragon *and wanted to talk to me about it. After we got our camper unloaded I returned his call.*

I ate cold supper that night because the call lasted for over an hour. Tom was a Wolfhound and served the same time as I. He had three or four things to say that I had not heard before. First, he said that the book was not only my story, but his. I had heard something close to that several times, but he went on to say that, no, he wasn't a farm boy, but a city kid. He said though he was raised completely different than me, we were the same. I understood. Tom told me several things he liked about the book and then said something I had not heard before. He said what the Dragon *was, was a love story. I said" What?" He said "Yes, a love story between a man and his country and a man and the soldiers he served with." I still consider that the finest compliment I've ever got about the book.*

Toward the end of our great visit he said "I guess I better tell you about a few mistakes I found in your book. I told him I knew there were mistakes because I was dealing with forty year old memory. "Oh, nothing big." He said "You know where you wrote at the end of your tour you went out reluctantly on a short sweep, but it didn't amount to too much and you weren't even involved with the short contact." Then he said that during that "not much of an action" is where he was critically wounded, and that short contact I wrote about was him.

The other thing was that it wasn't Ho Bo Woods, rather it was close to a place called Trang Bang. Of course, he would remember correctly, he was wounded there! It was December 20, 1966. Tom then asked where I was during the Bob Hope USO show on Christmas day. I told him about half way back in the audience (about 40 rows). He said he was the only stretcher there and he was laid down in front of the front row where all the walking wounded were. He said Joey Heatherton was there and Anita Bryant held his hand and talked to him and she was the most beautiful lady he had ever seen. The doctors operated on him the next day.

This is Tom Donovan's story in his words about:

Becoming a Wolfhound

I arrived in Vietnam on July 15, 1966. After several days pouring cement at Camp Alpha for new tent platforms they gave me orders for the 25th Infantry Division.

They loaded us in trucks and somewhere in the middle of nowhere the driver dropped me off at the only tent or anything else in the area with the orders to wait there until another truck would pick me up. I went into the tent and there were only two cots, 5 cases of C-Rations and some water. Soon after darkness came on and still no truck. I sat there all night, with no weapon watching flares going off and in the shadows I could see people out there. The good thing about jet lag is that I could not sleep even if I wanted to. I dared not smoke because I did not know what side those people out there were on.

The night lasted forever but somehow the sun did come up. Shortly after sun up trucks started to roll up and down the road but none stopped for me. Now the question started to come up. Did they really tell me to stay here or should I go and find someone who knew what was going on?

Morning came and went and still no truck. 1 pm, 2 pm, no truck. Finally about 2:30 a truck stops and the driver yells "Are you going to the 25th?" I jumped from the tent and ran screaming "Yes, yes, yes don't leave".

After an uneventful ride to Cu Chi I ended up at the 25th Replacement Company with several other replacements. The clerk starts to hand out our assignments when he says "who is Donovan?" I was hesitant to raise my hand but finally did when he says, "Boy are you screwed, you are going to the Second Wolfhounds." Actually, I don't think he said screwed. Anyway, that was my first sign of what was to come.

I was assigned to Company A, second Platoon, Second Squad. I was fortunate to have the best squad leader, SGT Max E. Goshorn, the best Platoon SGT, SFC Bernard Hoopii and the best Platoon Leader, 1LT Sam Awtry. Those three could be the reason I am alive today.

That evening we got mortared in Base Camp. Well, being the new guy that was my fault. The next morning we flew out to get the mortars and we landed in a hot Landing Zone. Again that was my fault.

Before flying out a very large man named Perrier walked up to me when I suited up and said "give me five dollars". I would have given him ten if he did not hurt me. Instead of beating me up he took a Polaroid picture of me in full gear and says "send this to your Momma so she can see what you looked like before you get your "f***in' head blown off". A great way to start my first operation.

Just like most of the replacements I did not have a name. I was just the "FNG" which we all know means the Friendly New Guy. I am not sure when I actually got my name back, but I did.

I served with these great Wolfhounds, great Warriors, great Americans and great Brothers until I was wounded on December 20, 1966. I was unfortunate to trip a land mine. Actually, it was a Booby Trap but I hate being the BOOB who tripped the trap so I call it a land mine. Most of us were draftees but no soldiers ever fought with more intensity that these men who answer the orders to report for duty.

As unfortunate I was, a NFG was assigned to me the night before. I got his equipment assigned and as we did not know we were going out in the field the next day I told him we would break him in later. Well they got us up to go on a mission so I told him to stick with me and I would keep an eye out for him. Well I got wounded in the legs and because he was sticking with me as I told him he got it in the chest. Some luck, here he was on his first mission for 2 hours and he was on his way home on a medevac.

When I left active duty, many years passed when I started to miss the camaraderie that only combat people can experience. Even if you did not like someone you would run through bullets to save him. That does not exist out in the world. When the 27th Infantry Regiment Historical Society was founded I joined right away. In the years that I have been a member I have been able to connect with several guys I served with. Even met my old company commander, LTG Robert F. Foley, who was CPT Foley when I was with him. Little Mikey Marcukaitis, Roger

Schoonover, Jim Hauser, Chuck Dean, Brothers then, Brothers now.

The friendships with all of my Brothers from Vietnam, my older Brothers from Korea and WWII and now forming friendships with my younger Brothers who are making the Wolfhounds proud today are some of the most precious friendships I hold today. I cannot imagine not seeing my fellow Wolfhounds a couple times a year.

I only served with the Wolfhounds for a short time but I feel that time helped form me to become the man I am today.

Once a Wolfhound, Always a Wolfhound. Tom Donovan

My entry into the Wolfhounds was pretty messed up but not nearly as confusing and disorganized as Tom's. I arrived Honolulu Oahu, Hawaii on a bright sunny July Sunday in 1966 and an Army bus hauled me to Schofield Barracks (about 20 miles from Honolulu airport) I knew even less than Tom about where to go and what was happening to me, but at least I was nowhere near a war! Midafternoon I walked into D Quad Barracks carrying my duffle bag and wishing I was home milking my cows. There were men just hanging around and everyone I walked by asked "Wolfhound?" I answered "I guess so" and I got replies from all of them with everything from "You'll be sorry!" to "Oh, you poor bastard". I reported to the orderly with some directional help from several of my new unit buddies. Even there I was greeted with the same. He said something like "Welcome to the 27th Infantry. I hope you like to work your ass off buddy." I was a 22 year old one stripe PFC and he was an old timer Spec 4 probably 20 years old so I figured he knew what he was talking about! But, like Tom Donovan, I soon learned we had the best officers and Non Coms in the Army. I immediately made lifelong friends and a few months later we would all be headed for Vietnam. Vietnam is where we learned what a really great unit the 27th Regiment was and why they worked us so hard in the Kahoka mountains in Hawaii. This old Mid-west farm boy had just crossed some of the Pacific Ocean! The biggest piece of water I had seen up til then was a 6 acre lake.

A Christmas Tale

Anyone that spent a Christmas in the military overseas, either in harm's way or not, has vivid memories of that time. I asked a few of the men that were in my Army unit for a memory of their Christmas in Vietnam. I knew I would get some good ones. Some would be tragic and some would surely be humorous. One of the guys told me about his best Christmas ever. He said he was due to leave for home soon (what we called being "short".) and absolutely did not want to go "out" on a mission. But, he was part of a patrol that was leaving the wire (base camp perimeter) two days before Christmas. They would certainly be would be out during and after Christmas day for sure. They were leaving the wire (perimeter of the base camp) and had not gone 50 yards when they called him back to the camp. His Sgt told him the truck for the airport was leaving in 20 minutes and he better be on it if he wanted to go home! The patrol went on out on their mission without him and he was on the truck!

Even though 40 plus years had passed, I knew these guys would remember well those days because I remember mine like yesterday. Good days or bad, we all remember Thanksgivings and Christmases without family.

I chose the following story that comes from Iowa from a good friend and a really great guy named ***Dave Hunt****. I'll let him tell the sort story in his words. But because he uses the slang that mostly only soldiers would understand, I should explain with a short glossary first. "Line" means in the field, sweeps and patrols. "Hooch" is a tent, house or cover. "Support bases" or FSP's or fire support bases are small outlying bases with artillery some distance from the main camp. He also failed to explain that his "fortunate" circumstance getting to leave the field was that he had been wounded for the third time. Also, "1st Wolfhounds" meant he was part of the 1st battalion of the 27th Infantry*

Regiment known as the Wolfhounds. I know it all sounds confusing, but that's the way Army guys talk.

Dave Hunt, Sgt Bluff, Iowa: A Christmas Tale

Dave Hunt taking a break in Vietnam

Dave writes,

Don:

My Christmas story begins about Dec. 15, 1968. I was very fortunate to get off line and become a Driver at 25th Div. Headquarters in Cu Chi Base camp. The drivers and orderlies stayed together in a hooch close to Headquarters, and we had a Christmas tree with lights. Being a driver, with the Bob Hope Troupe coming to Cu Chi., I was lucky enough to drive one of the performing cast members, and that enabled us drivers to enjoy front row seats at the show!

On Christmas Day Gen. Williamson visited every Support Base of the 25th Division. When it came time to go visit the 1st Wolfhounds at their FSB, I was invited to ride along, but to my despair my brothers of my Platoon were gone out on a mission when we got there and I missed them.

As far as stories from the field I usually like to think of the humorous ones. Such as, Co. D. or our Platoon was going out on night ambush or night roving patrol and RTO Merrill Sellers fell in one of those rice patty wells. Thank God we had the Company rope with us. Another time, Company D was on a 7 day operation and one of the days we stopped to set up ambush and eat our 7 course C-ration meal. I was hot, sweaty, mosquitoes and light rain falling. I was in real good positive mood. I laid my 79 across this path and just started enjoying my dinner and three Viet Cong on bikes run over my M79. Needless to say that got my attention. Anyway a short distance down the path one of our platoon Sgts was standing up relieving himself and the bike riders stopped to talk to him, he dove for his rifle, but needless to say he took a round in his rear cheek. Anyway these three Cong were point men for a whole company. Needless to say dinner was over with and a sleepless night was ahead.

Dave Hunt

John Shea, Junction, IL: Truck Driver

John was only one of five (I think) of the guys that trained together in Ft Leonard Wood that were sent to and stationed at Hawaii with the 25th Division. There were John Shea, Dennis Brugger, John Schmidt, Williams and myself. Out of a company of guys, our little group went to the Wolfhounds and the rest of the company was assigned to Germany and we never saw them again. Upon arrival at Schofield Barracks I was separated from the others with a different job. John Shea was attached to the motor pool and drove for the Wolfhounds his entire year in Vietnam, but we remained great friends then and still today.

I have several John Shea stories, but I'll give you one that meant a lot to "my squad". As the Division was trying to make Cu Chi look something military, conditions were primitive to say the least. The Division was all sleeping on the ground and there were no structures at all. Most of the guys had put ponchos on bamboo stakes and made a shelter of sorts. John Shea had been hauling ammo and supplies from an airbase near Saigon to the Wolfhounds area of course. It's about a thirty mile trip one way. John and his helper drove by an Air Force warehouse at Ton Son Nhut Air field and spotted a huge stack of military cots. They were stacked up all military style outside with no guards around. . We call them Army cots, but these were Air Force property. Since no one was around, John and buddy backed their truck up the stack, got out and loaded about fifteen of the soon to be Wolfhound beds. When they got to Cu Chi they drove down next to the wire where the Hounds were and pulled up by our platoon area and unloaded the cots. I know that don't sound like a big deal, but it was! Afterwards, when we were gone for a few days and came back, those cots were always still there. Amazing!

The Chaplain at Salt Lake

A uniformed man showed up at the reunion. An Army Major Chaplain currently serving and was invited to attend. I'm glad he was. Really a nice guy and he had a group around him most of the time he was there. He told of the many and varied problems of a Chaplain in a combat zone. I was among those there that hung on his words intently. There was a mini-reunion going on across the room about that time between a couple of guys that had not seen each other in 40 years. One of the guys in our group that saw this happening pointed it out to us. Of course that right there is what it's all about. There were lots of tears of course and that brought the Chaplin to tell a story. He told about an old soldier that had died and went to Heaven. As he was being shown around the place they came upon a barn and tools and such. The guide told him that this is where the old soldier would spend his day doing what he liked best. The old Soldier thought that was fine, but asked what that big pool over there full of water was for. The guide told him that that is the tears that were ready for him while he was on Earth, but he never used.

Rick Melli

I have known Rick Melli for 43 years. A more accurate statement would be that I've known of him for that long. I guess I've only really got to know him while in Salt Lake City at our '08 Wolfhound reunion. At previous reunions in the past 4 years I always spoke to him and called him Sir or Captain. I think we are about the same age or he may be a little older than I and that is a shame because he appears to be about 50 years old and is in great shape, unlike me and most of our counterparts.

This isn't the best story in these pages, but it means a lot to me. Captain Melli came up to me about the third day of the 2008 reunion and spoke to me and I replied, "Sir". He told me he wanted a word with me. We talked a while then went out in the lobby where there were not so much confusion and noise.

He asked me, "You know we're both civilians now, right?"

"Yes sir" I came back sharply.

"My name is Rick, not Sir or Captain either".

I sort of apologized then and offered a sort of explanation and told him I understood. He said then that calling him Captain would sure be wrong as he retired a Lt Colonel. I called him Rick then. What a great guy and what a great visit we had.

I learned a great deal in the next 30 minutes as we started talking about those times we shared over four decades ago. As these reunions go on year after year, one thing I am learning is that our Officers were people too. And more than that, they were people that cared. I started to suspect that fact after my first encounter with Sergeant Cary Clark at the Philly reunion in 2005 when he remembered me and said he remembered my best friend was a tall skinny kid from Tennesee. that died in Vietnam, but he couldn't quite call his name. I said "Charley Crowe?" And he said "right you are!" I couldn't believe someone in Command could hang on to something like that.

Anyway, back to "Rick". I told him that even though I was never close to any Officers I always somehow knew that we in the 27th had maybe the best officers the Army had to offer. I figured that when the brass somewhere noticed a really good officer, he was immediately assigned to the Wolfhounds. I said "Except, of course our XO, Major Lange" (Whom I did not care for). Captain Melli, I mean Rick, said," How about I tell you about Major Lange?" OK I say. "Major Lange was the 2nd Battalion Base Camp XO and he did his job just the way he was ordered to do it". Rick went on, "Don, when you rotated home, Major Lange signed for another tour and asked for a field leadership position. He was killed in action two months into his second tour."

From that I learned for sure, there are always two sides of every story and I guess we never know everything about what another man is made of. I certainly didn't "know" Major Lange. I have said unkind things about him in the past and I am now very sorry.

I was getting pretty comfortable talking with "Rick" by then and we then spoke of more personal feelings of the war for a time. Now I think of Rick Melli not only as a respected career officer, but just a really good guy too.

Gordon Maga: Gordie's Day at the VA

Gordie writes in his words:

The BEST DAY at the VA in a while happened today. I had an appointment 7:15 AM for a one tube scoop of blood, and then on my way home. As some of you know, but most of you don't, I have a small 200cc Dirt Bike. It is hand painted in Real Tree type Camo, along with the Helmet. Soooo....to save a little on gas I rode it to the VA. While I was getting my blood drawn, or should I say having them TRY to get my blood drawn, on the Sixth try a VA cop walked in the Room and said Mr. Maga we need you out front right now! I'll wait until they take the needle out of your hand. She pulled the needle out and told me to come back in when they were done with me. So the Cop escorted me out side to my bike where there were about 5 cops, around my bike.

"What's wrong?" I asked.

This little guy said, "ARE YOU some kind of Terrorist??"

I said, "What?" and started to laugh.

He said, "This isn't funny."

"Why?" I said.

"I went to write you a warning ticket for not parking in the proper area for motorcycles, when I noticed a bomb on your bike."

"A what?" I said.

"You're lucky you are not on your way to Guantanamo Bay!" I laughed again and they all said "This ain't funny." He said look, and low and behold I forgot to take the Grenade off the front fork of my bike. I explained that it was a dummy, and was on there for show. “Well, I was a former MARINE, and it made me crap my pants.”

I said, with a grin, “Pick it up and look at it. It's a look-alike.” I took it off, and gave it to him, he unscrewed the top and said to his buddies it’s ok, stand down. I took the ticket, and he wished me a good day, and I returned to the blood room and after 2 more tryies got my tube of Blood.

I told him as I left, “You have made my day."

“Why is that?” he asked.

“To have an Old Wolfhound like me make a young Marine like you s--- his pants, is by far the best thing that happened to me today!”

Lt Col William C. Barott

This is my Battalion Commander while in Vietnam. He was KIA at the same time as my friend Howard Barker. Howard was the RTO for the Col at the time. Col Barott was respected by all who knew him and served under him. Howard "Gater" Barker was a very good friend and one heck of a soldier. We had been together from the Hawaii training days and nearly 11 months of Vietnam. I miss him often.

Rank, Service Lieutenant Colonel O-5, U.S. Army Veteran of:

U.S. Military Academy 1947-1951

U.S. Army 1951-1966

Cold War 1951-1966

Korean War 1952-1953

Vietnam War 1966 (KIA)

Tribute:

William Barott was born on September 7, 1928, at Fort Sam Houston, Texas. He entered the U.S. Military Academy at West Point on July 1, 1947, and was commissioned a 2Lt of Infantry on June 1, 1951. Lt Barott completed Infantry School and Jump School before serving with the 38th Infantry Regiment of the 2nd Infantry Division during the Korean War, from November 1952 to December 1953. After Korea, Barott served with the 504th Airborne Infantry Regiment at Fort Bragg, North Carolina, from December 1953 to January 1957. Capt Barott next served as an Army ROTC instructor at Cornell University from September 1957 to September 1960. He then served with the 6th Infantry Regiment in Europe from September 1960 to July 1963. Barott served with the 82nd Airborne Division from July 1964 to December 1965, and then served with the Military Assistance Command in Vietnam as commander of the 2nd Battalion, 27th Infantry Regiment, 25th Infantry Division, from May, 1966 until he was killed in action on November 4, 1966.

The Army General Orders for his 2nd Silver Star reads:

For gallantry in action: Lieutenant Colonel Barott distinguished himself by heroic actions while commanding the 2d Battalion, 27th Infantry during Operation Attleboro, in the

Republic of Vietnam. Approximately fifteen miles east of Tay Ninh, the 1st Battalion, 27th Infantry was pinned down by exceedingly heavy fire in a densely wooded area. Lieutenant Colonel Barott's battalion was flown from Cu Chi to Dau Tieng as a reserve force. The Viet Cong began to make successive human wave assaults on the 1st Battalion. The 2d Battalion was committed to attack the flank of the pinned down battalion. Eagerly seizing the mission, Lieutenant Colonel Barott promptly organized his battalion for a helicopter lift into the objective area. Shortly after landing, he led his force into the dense jungle to attack the enemy flank which could be identified by the heavy firing. He was in radio contact with the commander of the beleaguered unit and all coordination had been completed. As he moved through the hot, humid terrain, a Viet Cong machine gun suddenly began firing at a very close range. The heavy vegetation of the jungle prevented prompt location of the gun, but Lieutenant Colonel Barott quickly organized his troops and began moving them around the line of fire. As he moved from man to man giving encouragement, the machine gun began firing again. However, this last fusillade enabled Lieutenant Colonel Barott to spot the exact location of the enemy weapon. He instructed the men on either side of him to load their weapons with fresh magazines and place fire on the Viet Cong gun emplacement. He then rose to lead the assault with the cry, "Let's go, Wolfhounds."

As he courageously led the charge in the face of insurmountable odds, Lieutenant Colonel Barott was killed by a heavy burst of fire from the machine gun. His unimpeachable valor and fearless leadership proved inspirational to the men of the unit. His gallant actions and heroic sacrifice reflect great credit upon himself, his unit, the 25th Infantry Division, and the United States Army.

Some Good Local Men

The next five guys I will describe are friends of mine that I have known most of my life. All are Vietnam vets serving at different times in the war with different outfits. Each of them holds great stories of their experiences in Vietnam including their return to the world. I mention the return, because many of the interesting and sometimes very humorous tales are of getting short, getting home or the arrival. One rule I started writing this with would be that all the stories I write would be about the Wolfhounds or of someone connected with the outfit. These will be a few of the exceptions. I will describe my connection with each before I tell their secrets.

Talking about coming home to the world. One guy told me that when he got back to his home town and met a good high school buddy. The buddy said, "Well, Don Osborn, where the hell you been? Haven't seen you for a spell!"

Bob Moles, Adrian, Missouri

Bob and I graduated from the same Midwest High school, but he was 4 years younger than I so he was a 65 grad. I got home to little Adrian Mo in early January 1967. I had been home only a couple of short days and was walking on the sidewalk on Main Street in Adrian, probably heading for my Mom's cafe for some free food. Bob yelled at me from across the street and came running over. I do not remember this encounter at all, but he has

told it many times, so it no doubt happened. He had a set of Army orders in his hand. I had not seen Bob since I had arrived home so I was surprised to learn he had been drafted and was out of AIT already. He showed me his orders and said he was headed for Vietnam real quick and could I give him advice that would help him. Like I said, I don't remember this, but he claims I said, "You bet Bob, look up, down, ahead and behind you all the time and stay awake". When he tells this, I always think I could have been a little more helpful than that, but I wonder what I could have said that would have prepared him for what he was about to endure. Probably nothing. Well, Bob was trained with and sent to Vietnam with the famous 23rd Infantry Division, more commonly known as the "Americal Division"

The first of the "Moles" stories takes place in a rice paddy during a firefight with the NVA that had escalated to the point that artillery was called in for support and a Marine detachment that was nearby doing an operation of their own was called in to help. The trouble started with a perfect ambush as the NVA was in spider holes and sprung the trap when the Americans were right on top of them. One of Bob's best friends (and still is to this day) was a big fellow named ***Jim Brewer*** *from a northern most county in Missouri. Big ol' corn fed farm kid he was. Jim was hit twice, once in the ankle and one round entered his shoulder and lodged in his chest. Medivac was needed badly for several* *wounded and soon a few dustoff choppers were landing and wounded were hurriedly being put aboard.*

On February 8, 1968 A Company of the 198th. L.I.B. (Light Infantry Brigade) was involved in a battle with NVA, known as the Battle of Lo Giang. Jim Brewer was wounded in that battle and laid in a paddy until a buddy, ***Mike Bonk*** *and a marine ran out to pull Jim to safety. The marine picked Jim up and carried him to a medevac chopper and tossed him in. The marine said, "If I'd known you were such a heavy son-of-bitch I'd have left you there". The chopper lifted off several feet, was hit by enemy fire and came back down. Jim said there were a few stressful moments wondering if they were going to get out of there, but the chopper lifted off again and carried the wounded to a mash unit. Jim spent 34 days on a hospital ship, several months in Japan, and finally back to a hospital in Colorado, U.S.A. He thanks* ***Mike Bonk*** *and the marine for saving his life. His one regret is that he didn't get that marine's name. One of Bob's favorite buddies he likes to tell tales about is a guy named* ***Alan Allen*** *from Allantown, Texas if one can believe that! First thing that Bob tells about him is while at an Americal reunion he attended he met Alan Allen for the first time in 32 years. What is so amazing about the meeting is the fact that Bob had believed Alan dead for all those years. He had witnessed Alan get wounded and loaded on* *the medivac Huey in such a condition that Bob assumed him terminal.*

Don Hammett, *another of Bob Mole's buddies, is a guy worth some words here too. He was the real joker in the unit (every outfit had one, I think it must have been a rule) and everybody liked him of course. He did two tours in Nam and then made a career in the Army. He even taught at a base in Mississippi.*

John "Chunky" Carlson *was wounded several times and almost every time a head wound! All the photos That Bob has of Chunky, He has bandages around his head someway. With a handful of Purple Hearts, he asked the CO if he couldn't get a different job somewhere as he was sure these wounds were an omen of some sort. It worked; Chunky was transferred along with his handful of Purple Hearts.*

Steve "Tator" Hubbard, Adrian, Missouri

Back row: Robert Sams, George McThemy, Herb Taylor.
Front: Steve Hubbard, Pete Mills

Steve is a 1964 grad from my high school and served two tours in Nam. He was then as now, very light framed man with no extra pounds hanging anywhere and standing at 5 foot six tall. Pound for pound, one of the best men I ever knew. He always reminds me of one of my best friends that I was with in Nam, Elmer French. I've carried pocket knives bigger than Elmer, but 100 percent dynamite he was (and no doubt still is)! I'm not sure where the nickname of Tator came from for Steve, probably because he's the size of a good bakin' tator.

About 2005 I was working in my store in Adrian Mo one day when a big fellow open the front door and walked in. Probably 55 to 60 years and at least six foot three. A real big fellow. I didn't recognize the guy and that is unusual in my small town not to know everyone. This big boy says to me, "They tell me you can give me the whereabouts of Steve Hubbard." Trying to be funny I asked him why anyone would want that guy. He said it was because Hubbard had carried him out of the jungle for over 100 yards and had surely saved his life. He said he had been critically wounded with small arms fire and would have died had it not been for Steve. For a guy Steve's size to carry this guy standing in my store any distance at all pretty well tells the kind of metal he is made of. The big guy's name was ***Sergeant Sams*** *and he had driven from his home in California to reunite with his old friend. I visited with this Sams guy while I ran Steve down and quickly decided that he was truly a remarkable man worth knowing.*

Steve Hubbard spent most of his time in the central highlands with the 4th Division. 1968 and 69. Steve served two tours in the Nam with his second tour being the most bazaar, fascinating and interesting. He was part of a six man team that lived with several hundred Monaguards in the Highlands in a Village called Plei

Brel Dor. They had about one hundred Mountain Yard soldiers under them and at their disposal in case of attacks. Steve was the senior EM and they did have a 1st Louie in command. Steve really liked the Mountain Yards saying that each one of them were worth ten ARVN any day of the week. He liked the people saying they were of high morals and very honest and always speaks well of them saying they were a brave and honest people.

Steve's MOS was Mortars, but never got to use that talent but very little during his tours. Anyway, there was an Army base camp not over ten miles from the village and Steve managed to appropriate for himself (that is steal in civilian talk) a 81 mortar and several rounds of WP, HE and some other types of ordinance for the thing, but, no sight as it was locked up and they found no aiming stakes. They had from time to time been probed by the enemy and a few times had been attacked fairly aggressively, but each time the small unit was able repel the assault. The NVA wanted to overrun the little village real bad. The acquisition of the mortar tube was a little added insurance needed for the group. Without aiming stakes and sights it was going to require some imagination to be of any value to them however. They dug the tube in and used a few rounds to visually zero in the target they felt most likely would become a threat. The enemy had always advanced on them from an old French fort on a ridge, so that became the focal point for new weapon.

Weeks went by before another attack, and then it happened.... The Mountain Yards saw movement and fired, and then the battle was on. Sure enough, the incoming ordinance was coming from the old fort, so Steve gets to try out their secret weapon. They start feeding the tube and hits were seen. About that time their radio starts screaming "Hold fire...hold fire, you're firing on Americans!!!!" No one had told the special little unit that their AO ended somewhere between the village and the old fort. The friendlies turned out to be an armored unit that had moved in to set up camp by the old fort. The unit was commanded by General Abrams' son! Steve had just fired on friendlies and it couldn't have been worse friendlies than a group commanded by the son of a World War II hero. For weeks Steve thought he would be court martialed (at the very least) but, evidently, since there were no casualties, nothing ever came of the incident.

Jimmy “Mertz” Kershner, Adrian, Missouri: LRRP

Jimmy was raised in Adrian, Missouri and after high school, the Army, Viet Nam and college, he has taught school in a town not far from where he was born. He graduated high school in 1966 in the same class as my wife, Sue. Mertz pulled two tours in Nam most of 69 through 71. His is a unique tale for sure. Those men that performed their duty showing indescribable valor have hair curling stories, but the job Jimmy did that amazes me the most is his time working LRRP (Long Range Reconnaissance Patrol).

Mertz worked with five other men in the boonies gathering intel and reporting what they found, avoiding contact with the enemy when possible. They were Airborne and did jump a few times into new AO’s, but when they jumped it was always at night. I'm not sure how tall of a guy he is. I'll guess him at 5 ft 5 and he may go 125 lbs today. Notice I said how tall and not how big a guy he was, thats because he is one of the biggest men I ever knew. He reminds me of Elmer (Em) French that I served in Vietnam with during 1966. When describing Em I always say he was the biggest little man I ever knew. This is also how I feel about "Merz" Kershner. The following are some of his stories and the first is about a kid they called ‘Babysan” and a night jump. ***It is written by Jimmy himself in his words.***

Babysan was hung up in a tree after a night jump. He couldn't see the ground at night, so the first thing to do is take the 75 ft rope we all carried as part of our equipment and lower a kit bag to find how high you are in the tree. Tex and I, by looking from the ground up, could see Babysan hanging in the tree. Instead of telling him he was only 6 ft or so up, we sat down and watched him go through all the effort of using the rope and lowering a kit bag. When he lowered the bag and realized he was only few feet in the air, Tex and I started giggling softly. When he heard us, Babysan was not happy, but he had to keep noise discipline, so he couldn't cuss us. A soldier has to have a little fun now and then.

FNG (F*** New Guy); Every trooper knows what this means, and how they can do the dumbest things. My 6 man LRRP (Long Rnge Recon Patrol) team had found a big NVA base camp. We reported the intel and hoped that would end our part. It wasn't. HQ sent out a Battalion of troops, and we were to lead 2 companies into the position. The plan was to get close, wait, then set up for a dawn attack. We got to a hold position, then I told the company COs to stop, put out security, and have their people chow down and rest. I walked back down the trail checking security. Off the trail in the bush, I could see the top of a guy's helmet. I stepped toward him, and I could see he was eating. A FNG can always be identified by how he eats his rations. Experienced boonie rats open a can, eat it, then open more, eating one can at a time. FNGs open several cans taking a bite at a time like eating a meal off a plate. This FNG had his cans laid out to eat, but he was using an unexploded aerial bomb as a table. If it exploded, we were all dead. As calmly as possible, I told him to freeze. I told him he was eating off a bomb. He looked at me, and I saw the dawn of comprehension in his eyes. I told him not to move until I told him to. I went back up the trail getting everyone up and moved a safe distance. I then preformed the bravest (or dumbest take your pick) act of my time in combat. Instead yelling for him to come up the trail, I went back and got the guy. I didn't cuss the kid, and I was proud of my self control. The guy was drenched in sweat and badly scared. Nothing I could say to him could have made him feel any worse than he already felt. I just told him that he had found out what it meant to be badly scared, but he controlled his fear and learned to deal with it.

We made a successful attack the next morning. After the fire fight, I looked the guy up. He was OK and had done his job with his squad. He wasn't a FNG anymore.

Even in combat guys have to have a little fun, but it seemed my guys were a little weird when it came to what they considered humorous. We were set up for a chopper extraction. I was on the LZ bringing the chopper in, and my 5 guys (we were a LRRP team) were hiding in the tree line. I heard and saw a commotion in the bush from their position. The chopper hovered, and the guys came running out of the tree line, but they looked strange while running. They were running in a single file and close together. When they got to the chopper, I saw that they had a huge snake (12 ft python) they had killed. They were carrying the snake like it was a piece of pipe. They jumped on the chopper with the snake. The chopper pilot was going crazy; My guys were laughing and flipping off the pilot; and I was yelling to get the chopper off the ground. We went into LZ Uplift. Uplift was new at that time, and people were housed in bunkers, but the REMFs were in big wall tents with electric lights. That night the guys had a great time with their snake. They would sneak into a tent, lay the big snake out between the bunks, flip on the lights, and yell "SNAKE!" The REMFs would tear the tent apart trying to get out. The guys had a good time for a while, but then the snake started to stink. As I said, my guys' idea of humor was a little different. Like the time Tex burned down the Officer's Club on LZ Uplift, but that is a story for another time.

Anyone who has ever served in a combat zone will tell people that a person runs the whole gamut of human emotions. Everyone understands that mind-numbing fear is a part of war, but the amount of humor, compassion, and pity that abounds in a combat unit can come as a surprise to people. One of my favorite memories of Vietnam happened in a road ditch on Highway 1, a few miles south of the Bong Song River. My LRRP team had walked out of the mountains down to the Highway. We radioed in our location and instead of a chopper, they sent out a truck to pick us up. While we were waiting, a Vietnamese woman and her daughter of about 10-11 years old came walking down the road. She was carrying 2 baskets of produce balanced on a stick across her shoulders. Even though it was a woman and child, we watched them closely as they passed. We greeted her (in Vietnamese); she replied and kept going. One of the guys remarked that she looked pregnant to him. As it turned out, she was very pregnant. She went about 50 meters past, then stopped, sat down, and leaned back against the side of the ditch. The five of us turned and looked at the sixth member of our team. He was our team medic. He was a fast talking guy from Louisiana. Naturally we called him Cajun.

Army field medics are highly trained individuals, but we doubted that Cajun had much training in birthing babies. He was going to get some OJT (On the Job Training). We walked down to the woman, and Cajun started barking orders at us, but spoke soothingly to the woman. Cajun got our cleanest towel and prepared to help the woman while 5 very nervous troopers watched and did what we were told. The woman was probably the calmest one there. The baby was born (a girl). Cajun tied the umbilical cord with a boot lace, and I cut it with a K-Bar jungle knife. Babysan (team RTO and youngest member of the team) brewed the woman a cup of tea and gave her a cigarette. After her tea and smoke, the woman gave the baby, wrapped in a towel, to her daughter, picked up her baskets, and headed down the road to town. This was one very tough woman.

I have thought often of this day. If this little girl is alive today, she would be over 40 and probably have grown children of her own. I like to think that she has told her children of how she was born in a ditch, helped along by one very fine US Army medic as 5 very nervous, hard-case troopers looked on. A moment of humanity in the middle of a war.

Jimmy “Mertz” Kershner

Tom Pullen, Creighton, Missouri: Artillery Man

Tom Pullen resting on a bunker

Tom was an artillery man with the 1st Cav mostly serving in the Corp III area so he wasn't very far from Cu Chi. He was a 155 man normally set up in fire bases with a company of infantry around for added protection. Tom served with B/1/30th FA, 69-70, CPL Guns. Fire Base Carolyn was fairly typical as bases go. They had 3 155's, 3 105's a 4 duce mortar team and one quad 50 mounted on a duce and a half. They did have the company of infantry and they rotated platoons of that company running patrols around the little base.

Tom and his wife live in a little town not more than a stone's throw from my town and we attend the same Church. I needed to include his story in this project for several reasons. He is a fine Christian man for whom I have great respect. He is a combat artillery Vietnam veteran and he continually praises the infantry while humbly dismissing his own contribution.

Artillery men all have a few things in common. Number one, of course is none of them can hear it thunder. None of them got a full night's sleep very often and the demand for missions around the clock was constant. Tom continues to say that everybody in Nam had it rougher than him. I think that is a fairly common statement from most vets, that they sure wouldn't have wanted this or that job. Tom's battery was involved in hair raising battles more than few times of course; this one in particular involves humor along with tragedy. It was at a Fire Base called "LZ Carolyn" and took place on 6 May of '69.

Starting out at the beginning of the NVA attack, all the guns of the entire battery were elevated at high angle just as they are designed to be used. After a long, loud and confusing battle, things started going the NVA's way and the big American guns were all lowered to point blank elevation. They were firing everything they had and exceeding the recommended rate of fire for artillery pieces. The fear being if the rate is exceeded the gun gets so hot that it can ignite the next charge as it is chambered killing the good guys. All during this, a man named Corporal **Jerry Peck** *from Hudsonville, MI had been rolled out of bed and into the fray while in boxer shorts and untied boots. He had stripped down airing out and was literally caught napping when the attack began. After all but him in his gun grew had been taken out of the action, he was running his gun by himself. He was* *cutting powder, loading and firing as fast as he could. A nearly unbelievable feat and all in his skivvies! The NVA then got inside the wire and behind the guns. As the Fire Base was being overran, chaos and havoc rained for a long time. Infantry and artillerymen, using every weapon they had, finally won the day.*

These gun crews are all taught to be any part of the crew at any time and at the time of this particular action, Tom was ammo dude. Spec 4 Tom Pullen left his gun to run after more bee hive rounds for his 155 and as he was making a beeline to the stored ammo he hurdled what he thought was a dead NVA laying on the ground. A few steps passed the expired enemy he saw Sgt Crabtree turn more toward Tom and fire his M16 at what looked like point blank at Tom himself. Tom turned and looked behind himself to see the NVA soldier falling back. Sgt Crabtree had just saved the life of Tom Pullen for the NVA had Tom in his sights and ready to fire when Tom's Sgt took him out. For action that day, Tom Pullen and **Jerry Peck** *were both recommended for the Silver Star with valor. The Captain said that only one man would get it and it was Tom's friend Corp Jerry Peck. Tom Pullen says that the Jerry deserved the medal because he ran his gun by himself and he was not dressed for combat while he did it!*

Tom told me that the LT that always told them never to exceed the recommended rate of fire was yelling the whole time to move faster! All of a sudden over 10 rounds a minute seemed like the thing to do.

Bob Brewster, Adrian Missouri: Wolfhound Tough

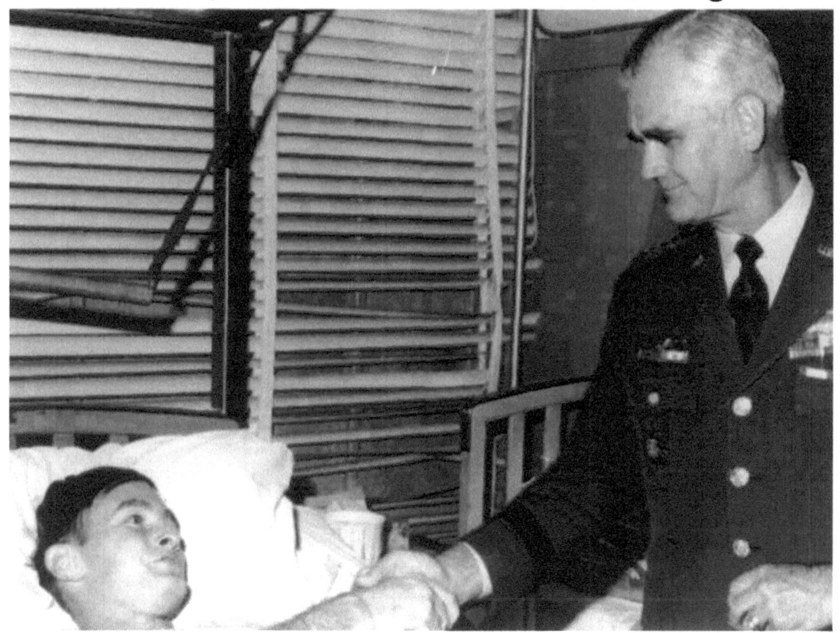

Bob Brewster and General Westmoreland. Bob receiving his Purple Heart.

Following is a short story I wrote about a friend of mine named Bob Brewster. The story was published in the Wolfhound newsletter/magazine that is called the "Wolfhound Pack" in the winter of 2011.

By Don Arndt

Being successful in everything a Wolfhound starts isn't anything unusual. Also, stories of great accomplishments from everything from the battlefield to the civilian workplace will not surprise any Wolfhound, present day or past. But I want to tell about a special friend of mine that I knew long before he joined the 27th Infantry.

Bob Brewster grew up on a farm a few miles from me and we graduated from the same small town Mid-West Missouri high school. Even though I am four years his senior, being such a small town, everyone knows everyone. I returned home from Vietnam in January 1967 and started my life in the world. Bob entered the Army in 1969 and I got to visit with him just before he left. When he arrived in Vietnam, he was immediately sent to the 2nd Bat 27th at Cu Chi where he joined C Company 3rd Platoon. On 19 August 1970, while on patrol in Ho Bo Woods, Bob tripped a booby trapped 105 round and lost a leg. After a year in the VA hospital healing his many wounds and having the remaining leg they saved fused at the knee, he finally got to come home to Adrian, his family, and his farm. His wife decided she didn't want to be married to a "cripple" and was not there when he got home. So here's the Wolfhound tough part that probably won't surprise many old Hounds. Bob started up his farm again, only this time with hand operated John Deere tractors and combines. Of course, being the good mechanic he is, he fixed them all up himself so he could operate them. Bob remarried and with his beautiful wife of 30 years, Barbara, at his side, he still runs 75 head of beef cattle and builds his own fence, etc. Bob never complains and when asked about the loss of the use of his legs he just says, "Hey, I just had a bad day". Oh yes, working a farm isn't quite enough for Bob, so for 20 plus years he has driven a rural mail route of 120 miles with 400 stops, five days a week. He uses a Chevy S10 with hand controls. That job alone is a good hard eight hour work day.

So I have been trying to get him to a reunion ever since my first one in Philly. Like the rest of us, he didn't know what to expect and was apprehensive to say the least. Bob and Barbara did attend the Branson reunion this year. He hooked up with some Charlie Company guys and had some great visits with many of the other Hounds. Bob called me a few days after we got home and said to me, "Don, for the first time, I felt like I had come home."

Back to Wolfhound Buddies

John Babbitt, Houghton Lake, Michigan

John Babbitt sits with his M60 Machine gun

Right on Through

John is one of those men that everybody likes at the first encounter. I missed being with John in Vietnam by almost two years as he arrived in country and joined the wolfhounds during September 1968 (the year of the TET offensive). I had left December 30, 1966. However, we were both Wolfhounds, but we had much different experiences. The war had changed, the enemy had changed and the way the US Army was taking care of business had changed. But the Wolfhounds have never changed.

That special attitude, that feeling, that pride just never wavered. The Wolfhounds in Iraq have the same air about them as those in WWII, Korea and Vietnam. Their tactics and weapons will evolve, but always they will have that thing inside them that they all have had before them, that thing we can't exactly describe, but that thing that makes them go a little farther and do a little more than 100%.

My wife and I first met John and his wife, Sherry, at my first Wolfhound reunion in Philadelphia several years ago. That special bond that Vietnam vets have had some to do with it, but seconds after we met I felt we were "brothers," truly brothers. I'll tell you some of what I've learned from this modest and very spiritual man.

John was a drafted kid from Michigan and West Virginia and other places he says, but is really "from" West Virginia. He and his wonderful wife were married after his AIT just before he left for the war. Now, these guys that were married in Vietnam had some more of a load to carry than everyone else. The strain of worrying about their life partner back home wore on them and you could see it in their faces constantly.

John and Sherry's union was evidently a good one proven by the fact that after 44 years they are still in love and together.

I asked John for his story and I was glad he gave it to me. His is like many who went into harm's way for their country, but ended up doing what they did mainly for their buddies.

Most will tell the funny stories first and that is what John did as he started with Karl. Karl was the M 79 man. This weapon shot a big, heavy round the size of a grenade. A single shot, very deadly machine by any standards. He, like all "79" men, carried lots of ammo for this contraption in a bag sometimes weighing 50 plus lbs and when coupled with the already heavy gear it made him really heavy. After one operation the men were running to a slick to evacuate an area when Karl ran into the chopper and his momentum carried him straight through the machine and out the other side. He managed to get control, pick himself up and back on board before lift off. Of course that was a belly laugh moment for all and a good story to bring up many times later. Even 40 years later.

John Babbitt was lucky. He headed into this war with buddies that he had gone through both basic and AIT with. They were all drafted from the Detroit area. Many guys arrived alone and having a buddy along made all the difference. They went over to 1st Cav and the rest went to the Wolfhounds.

They all had a 15 day leave before their departure for Vietnam and agreed to meet for the flight to San Francisco, California. One of the group, **Fred Cox,** *had this great idea, "Why don't we* *take an extra 4 days." Great idea and then it was said, "What can they do, send us to Vietnam?" That was good for John because he was getting married while on leave. When they finally arrived in San Francisco they decided to take one more day off there as well. Well, no harm done and no punishment when they finally arrived. All that was said was that they each had pay coming and since John was married, he had to fill out some extra papers and then off to war they went.*

John arrived in Vietnam in September 1968. It was after the major offense the enemy had mounted during TET of that year. By comparing stories from "old timers", TET had changed everything in the way things were done. John arrived at Tan Son Nhut Airfield a newly married man not really knowing what to expect in this blistering hot, stinking new land.He was immediately assigned to the 25th Division (Tropic Lightning) based at Cu Chi. When He got there he started a one week indoctrination course training the newbies a little more on Vietnam. He was assigned to ***Company D of the 1st Battalion of the 27thRegiment*** *"Wolfhounds" of that Division (1/27th). Part of that "school" was an AP (ambush Patrol) on the out side of the wire. The temporary team/squad went out 100 meters and set up out in the open in the camp's open and cleared fire lane where it had been defoliated. They didn't go as far as the jungle this first time out. This was practice for the new guys. Some of the class* *included a map reading refresher courses and such. After school was over each were assigned to their respective squads and that's where John first met one of his new life long friends,* **Dave Hunt.**

John joined lots of new people that he soon started "learning." He met **Dave Hunt**, **Karl Shepard** *and* **Ed Bryson** *and* **Ben Frankel**, **Tom "Curley" Boyles, Robert Herrimgton.** *These men would soon become his family, and with them 24/7, working with them day after day. John is no different than most of the Vietnam vets that you try to get stories out of. They have lots to say about the things their buddies did and said, but little about themselves. It is pretty common that they all believe their buddies were the heroes and on their own behavior under fire, they "just don't remember."*

First wound

October '68, during a mortar attack, John was hit with shrapnel. He had small pieces in his scalp, back and left leg. Like many men, he carries some of these today. John had a boil on his left knee at the time that had become badly infected, but not wanting to be accused of goldbricking, had not complained. The Doc said when he looked at all of the wounds told John that him getting hit saved his leg. If he had waited a few more days he would have the lost leg from infection.

John's first Platoon leader in Vietnam was Lt Jay Frietas who was also wounded in that attack. They never saw each other again til that great Wolfhound reunion in Philly when they and John's last Platoon leader, Lt Don Yates all hooked up after all those years.

Ambush patrol

John was one of a few on AP (ambush patrol) not a long way from the wire (camp perimeter). They had moved in a circular path, swung back parallel and had gotten about 300 meters deep into the jungle past the edge of the cleared fire lane. They heard the blump…blump of a motor tube pretty close and then heard the voices of the enemy that were working the tube. The enemy was set up between them and the Fire Base and they were firing on the Fire Base. ***LT Yates*** *called in artillery on the bad guy mortar position and everything quieted down after that. They weren't there very long at all until* ***Karl Sheppard*** *had to wake up* ***John and Ed Bryson****, telling them that they could fall asleep faster than anyone he knew they were snoring so bad that he was afraid they were going to give away their position. They wound up spending the night in that location and never made it to the planned ambush site.*

Best point man in Nam

When John Babbitt first started working with this new family he had joined, they started out on a patrol and Ed Bryson told John not to worry, Curly Boyles is on point. He smokes a lot of pot, but never while he's on point, He's the best there is at walking point!

The following in John's words:

Albert "Cookie" Cook

Cookie was cleaning some claymores up and had pulled the detonator blasting cap out of one. He was cleaning it and it blew up in his face. It burned him so bad that it left so many "pot marks" all over his face you would have thought it was from a grenade, not a little blasting cap. Cookie said they had to scrub his face with a wire brush to get all the metal out.

I Quit

A little about **"Curly" Boyles**, a very funny guy. When things were bad, maybe as bad as they could get, Curly would just declare, 'I resign!" Sometimes he would exclaim that he was just going to quit right then and go home. Another favorite exclamation was that, "Well Damn it, now my hair is all messed up".

Joe the New Guy. He Just Wants to Go to the Field

This next short story about an encounter with one certain soldier was written by John Babbit in his own words.

I don't know the name of the guy. We went out on Eagle Flight to some village across the river from FSB Malone and he was on one of the choppers that picked us up. The story was that he was a clerk back at Division and wanted to see combat. Guess he was persistent in his request and a drinker that would get even more persistent when he drank. He finally aggravated someone with authority enough that he got his wish.

He was at the least enjoying a "good buzz" when he got to us and had a bottle of hooch with him and was willing to pass it around. He had a few takers and seemed to be about the happiest fellow any of us had seen in Viet Nam. Seems we weren't really needed where we were at and after cooling our heals for a couple hours we were ordered to our PU (Pick Up) zone.

I guess someone wanted to teach him a lesson about what being a grunt was all about and stuck him out on flank for our little hike to the PU zone. The village we had just left seemed so peaceful and friendly that I don't think anyone thought Charlie was anywhere near us. That was usually when something happened...when you least suspected it.

I remember seeing a "coolie hat" pop up out of the ground to my left where "Joe the new guy" was walking flank. All I saw was a flash, less than a second, of that coolie hat popping up and then it was gone, but one shot from an AK rang out and "Joe the new guy" was dead. You know I may have seen that flash of coolie hat after the shot was fired, not sure after 41 years. I do know I didn't see it long enough to react and remember thinking that I wish I would have had time to open up on it with my M-60.

He was tagged and bagged and we continued to the PU zone. Nobody was laughing anymore at the drunk antics of "Joe the new guy." it was dead quiet the rest of the hike, right up to the time we entered the PU zone and the first lift was coming in, then we got hit with a lot of small arms fire. The fire continued until the 2nd lift, the one I was on, came in. That was when **Karl Sheppard**, the 79 man in our squad, was running so fast for our chopper that he jumped in that bird and flew right out the other side. I remember we all got a good laugh out of how comical he looked. Guess Karl took our minds off "Joe the new guy" cause I don't think we ever mentioned him again

Tropic Lightning Soldier

John Babbitt was chosen "Tropic Lightning Division soldier of the day" and was given a stand down back at Cu Chi base camp. Kind of a thank you for job well done. This break, offered to two soldiers picked, was the brainchild of 25th Division commander

General Williamson. Why it was called "Soldier of the day" when they picked two, only the Army could answer that one.

He was picked up by General Williamson his personal chopper and flew to Cu Chi and given quarters to stay in. He was given PX opportunity, hot chow, showers and clean clothes. When he got in and landed at the helipad he met Dave Hunt who had been wounded three times and given base camp duties because of the three Purple Hearts. Dave was wounded his third time the day that John was wounded the first time. John had not seen him since he was transferred and his great friend had been given the driver job for General Williamson. The General told Dave to drive John where he needed to go in his jeep.

One of the unexpected treats was the meal with General Williamson. John describes him as a very Spiritual man and remembers that the man said grace before they all ate.

Overrun at the Battle of Dau Tieng

The battle lasted from the night of February 21, 1968 until the afternoon the 22nd. This was during the Vietnamese observance of TET.

The company had been out for several days in the bush and had a break coming, so they were allowed to stand down at the base at Dau Tieng. The 1st Battalion was headquartered there at the time. That night after they had all got settled down for a much needed catch-up of sleep, as they say, all hell broke loose at the wire. **Jimmy Antrobius** was the one that woke everyone up in the hootch. The whole platoon was in a hootch by the airstrip. The good guys' base camp was under attack and it was a big one. Most of the men in the bunkers had stripped down to their skivvies in an attempt to air out. The guys scrambled to put on some clothes and gear. John grabbed his M-60 (machine gun), a few belts of ammo and ran outside with **Jimmy, Ed Bryson, Karl Sheppard, Ben Frankel and Robert Herrington** that only moments before had been enjoying the rest and quiet. The NVA were already inside the wire because sappers had blown three line bunkers in a row which killed or wounded their inhabitants before they could react to the onslaught. That let a big hole open up for the NVA to funnel through. The artillery flares were lighting the area well enough to see that the place was swarming with NVA.

LT Yates was caught on the other side of the air strip so John's group had no orders and no leader in charge. The small group could see lots of figures moving inside the wire, the NVA was mixed in with friendlies and John was afraid to open up with the 60 for fear of killing good guys. John then suggested they move close to the wire to "plug" up the hole as the NVA were still coming through. Just then they spotted a bunch of NVA down in and along a ditch by the wire. John opened up with the 60 and it immediately had a stoppage. Two rounds tried to chamber at once and all John needed was a bayonet to dislodge it, but like everyone else caught off guard, he had no bayonet or anything to fix it with. So John pulled his .45 pistol and commenced to do battle. That's right, no clip in it.

About this time two APC's (Armored Personnel Carriers) rolled up and just as they turned to head toward the breach in the perimeter, they both blew up from satchel charges and were disabled. This was rapidly becoming a situation where everything that could go wrong… was. John's fellow bunk mates were doing OK with their M 16's but John was momentarily out of the fray. About then, the artillery pieces shot more parachute flares and they were going off overhead lighting up the place like day. Just then one of the engineers came up to the small group with a case of grenades. The men immediately started pitching them into the enemy, but not one of them went off. Soon they started coming back from the bad guys, but this time they were working just fine. Thankfully every one of the returning grenades was falling short. More flares, more noise and chaos everywhere. One of the guys noticed that all the grenades had a safety wire around them. That was the trouble. The enemy had figured it all out quick enough, but this new trick with the grenades took a while for the Wolfhounds to figure out in the dark, the noise of battle and the confusion.

With that little mishap corrected, the battle continued. About then is when a sapper got close to a bunker that the men had formed up next to, he threw his satchel charge toward the observation slit in the bunker. The charge missed the hole and detonated after it bounced back off the bunker next to the good guys. This killed the sapper, but wounded a few of the guys including John whose left eye was injured.

He left Vietnam in March and that was the end of the war for John. He spent the next several weeks in hospitals as they tried to save his eye. He eventually lost his eye from the wound.

This battle was when Jimmy Antrobius's got his third purple Heart and John earned his second. Both of John's wounds came at the same time as two of Jimmy's. John spent a week in the hospital in Japan, and then was transferred to an Army hospital in Valley Forge General in Phoenixville, Pennsylvania.

Before he left to go to the Army, the workers at his job had presented him with a small Bible to keep with him. He kept it in an old ammo box so the weather and elements couldn't get to it. **Bryson** sent all his stuff to him from Nam, but the Bible he treasured so much wasn't among the items.

My New Buddy

This is me and my new buddy.

In one of our evening stops and I don't remember where, about dusk after we were dug in for the night, a Vietnamese boy came into our camp. I don't even remember what time of the year it was other than it wasn't raining, so it was probably in February of 1966. This little guy just walked into the camp and looked around. I had just opened a can of rations as he walked by me. I handed him some of what was still in my C box and he sat down with me and we had supper together. We were buddies by then. He spoke only a little English, but we communicated enough. He was fascinated with the Wolfhound crest with the dog on it. I made him understand that was what we all were called. He thought that was very funny. He then claimed he was one too and I guess that was when he began making his plans. The next morning he was still there right beside me and as we were all saddling up to move he explained how he was going with us. Of course that was impossible, but he kept insisting that he was a "Wolfhound" too as he pointed to himself! I've since forgotten his name, but I will never forget the boy. How quickly we became close.

Larry "Cam" Campbell and the Lady

Cam was from Johnson City, Tennessee. One of those slow talking, fast thinkin southern boys and one of my best all time friends. We were stationed in Hawaii together and went to Vietnam together as well.

The lady came into one of our one night camps. I'm not sure if she thought she was ready to give birth and needed help or what, but she acted as she needed help. Maybe she simply wanted the safety of our group and something to eat. Whatever the reason she came there, big hearted Cam gave her his rations and they became friends for those few hours. Sometimes I think I remember

Cam and some of us helping her deliver, but I'm just not so sure that happened anymore. Cam was a fine soldier and had a heart big as all outdoors.

Roger "Dodger" Cates, Greensboro, NC

Some of the guys are very closed mouthed even to each other and this next man is one of those. But in few words he makes clear a common message.

This is Roger "Dodger" Cates, 2/27th Wolfhounds Vietnam 1966

...trapped in a time capsule is what I often feel, from a warrior's perspective. The mentality of war never fades from my soul. There is a poem written by William Soutar that goes...

No Man Outlives the Grief of War ...
Although He Outlives It's Wreck...
Upon the Memory,
a Scar Through All His Year's Will Ache.

I can relate to what is witnessed by our current soldiers, in that most of the civilian populace doesn't have a clue about what is required in being a combat soldier. The sacrifices, the distance created from family, the stories told ...falling on deaf ears. Does anyone really care what today's soldier life is really like? Is patriotism dead, and apathy lives on, or just on the back burner? It's the story of the sheep, sheepdog's and wolves. As long as the sheepdogs do their business, the sheep continue to sleep...and so it goes down in history...the song remains the same, for those on the perimeter...

Dick Siebel, Cedar Falls, Iowa

Dick Siebel

"Spec 4... Company commanding sir"

I wish everyone had a chance to meet this guy. I have had the pleasure at several of the reunions and have learned to admire him and his family both. Dick is a Christian man with a great "up" attitude that lights every room he is in. I never knew him in the war, but we were there at the same time, only he was with the sister Battalion (the First Bat) of the Wolfhounds. I may have even seen him in passing in Vietnam, but who knows. I got the following letter from him a few years ago shortly after a reunion that was held in Louisville, KY. Since then we have had several great visits.

Don,

You don't know me, but I was in Vietnam at the same time that you were. I was there from Feb 1966 to Feb 1967. I was in Charlie Company 1st Battalion, 27th Infantry, 25th Infantry Division.

My wife and I were at the Wolfhound Reunion in Minn. and Kentucky. Dorsey Weeks gave me your card and pointed you out in Kentucky, but it was late the last night and I didn't get a chance to talk to you. Dorsey was in my unit in Nam.

The reason I am writing is that I purchased your book, and read it cover to cover, but some of it was very difficult to read. I have a hard time with things about Vietnam as I have PTSD, undiagnosed until I retired and had all that time on my hands.

Reading a lot of your book was like reading about myself. I didn't live on a farm in Missouri, but I lived in a small country town in Iowa, Population 44. I worked on a farm all through High School.

I didn't know my buddies in Nam as well as you because I didn't know them for very long. I joined the Wolfhounds shortly after they arrived in Vietnam. I carried a M79 grenade launcher for the first six months, and then one day the First Sgt. came over and asked if I would like to be the Company Commander's RTO. So the last of my time in Nam I carried a radio.

Only one thing that I noticed wrong with your timeline was Attleboro started on the 3rd of Nov. 1966. The reason I know this is that our company was the one in big trouble that you had to come out to help, and I was the first one wounded that day. Our CO and First Sgt. were both killed. I ended up in command of the company for the rest of the day. I received the Silver Star and Purple Heart for action on 3 Nov 1966.

When I returned home I, like you, was one of the lucky ones. My wife is one of the greatest women a man could ever want. She put up with a lot of stuff from me that nobody else probably ever would have. She stuck by me through all my problems with PTSD even when I didn't know there was a problem. She is my life and I couldn't live without her.

I couldn't believe it when I read that the only movie that you couldn't sit through was “We Were Soldiers”. I walked out of the theater before it was even one quarter over. I bought the DVD, determined to make it through it. It took many times and a lot of support from my wife and my kids, but I made it through, but I don't think that I could sit down right now and get through it again. Just too hard.

My wife, by the way her name is Dixie and mine is Dick, and I are planning to make it to Salt Lake City next year. We didn't know that they were having reunions until I found Dorsey on the Internet and he told me about Minn. We are going to try to make all of them if we can. As I said earlier we were at Minn. and Kentucky. Perhaps you saw us. We kind of stand out a little. My wife, right now has to have a wheelchair for long distances. She uses a walker for short distances. We are working on eliminating both of them. So we were the ones with the wheelchair.

I guess I should sign off for now, but wanted to let you know I enjoyed your book even though it was emotionally hard to read. If you have any questions, please feel free to contact me. You have my e-mail, snail mail, and telephone.

Wolfhounds Forever, Dick Siebel

So, following is a copy of the orders awarding Dick the Silver Star.

HEADQUARTERS
25TH INFANTRY DIVISIDN
APO San Francisco 96225
GENERAL ORDERS 9 January 1967
NUMBER 101
AWARD OF THE SILVER STAR

l. TC 320, The following AWARDS are announced,

SIEBEL, RICHARD J. US5583769E SPL B-h

Co C, lst Bn, 27th Inf, 25th Inf Div

Awarded: Silver Star

Date action: 3 November 1956

Theater: Republic of Vietnam

Reason: For gallantry in action: Specialist Four Siebel distinguished himself by heroic actions on 3 November 1966, while serving as a radio operator for the Company Commander of Company C, lst Battalion, 27th Infantry on this date the company was air-lifted into a jungle area long known to be a Viet Gong strong-hold: As the company advanced, it came under murderous automatic weapons fire from the front and right flanks. As the company commander moved throughout the battle area, Specialist Siebel was always at his side monitoring all communications. Early in the battle he was wounded in the leg by small arms fire, but refused evacuation and continued to move with the company commander, 'When the company commander was fatally wounded, he moved him to a more secure area and started first aids. With complete disregard for his own personal safety, he carried the company commander through an open area to the approaching helicopter, which was surrounded on two sides by snipers with automatic weapons. Upon departure from the landing zone with the wounded, the helicopter was shot down, Specialist

Siebel returned to the area and retrieved the company commander. Specialist Siebel also rendered calm and precise reports to the battalion commander appraising him of the situation until another officer assumed command. As the battle terminated and all wounded were evacuated. Specialist Siebel again refused evacuation He remained with the company during the next twenty four hours during which the company was again engaged in heavy fighting. Specialist Siebel's personal courage and his great loyalty are in keeping with the highest traditions of the military service and reflect great credit upon himself, his unit, the 25th Infantry Division; and the United States Army. Authority: By direction of the President under the provisions of the Act of Congress approved 9 July 1918, and USARV message 16699. 1 July 1966.

Matthew "Frenchie" Kritzer

Matthew Kritzer with his M60 machine gun

Matthew joined up in the Army in Columbus, Ohio. He arrived in Vietnam Nov. 24, 1966 and traveled back to the world Nov. 24, 1967 He came over with Company C, 2/3rd Infantry, 199th Light Infantry Bde. He was hospitalized during May in Saigon. When he was released he was reassigned to 1st squad, 3rd Platoon, Co.B, 1st Bn, 27th Infantry, 25th Inf Division.

Matthew tells me he was nicknamed "Frenchie" because he spoke fluent French due to his Mom being French. He came from a long line of warriors; Grandpa was French Foreign Legion wounded in WWI, Dad was a Medic with 1st Div., second wave on Omaha Beach, Grandma and Mom both worked for the FFI French Underground during the war. He had dual citizenship but grew up in Paris until 7th grade, then lived in Columbus, Ohio. Frenchie was awarded two bronze stars with the Wolfhounds, one for merit, one for valor.

The following is Frenchie's very touching story of his best buddy. A buddy he lost in Vietnam a long time ago.

Forgive and forget the wilderness of horrors. Vietnam is now just a glossy photograph in the American Journal. But my photographs cannot be touched up; the memories don't erase that easily. When I stumble across a photograph of my best friend and I look into his eyes, I know that forgetting is totally out of the question. Now, just a fading yellowing photograph, shuffled among a myriad of others, he lays somewhere in a drawer; doomed not to be found on purpose or often. Dog-eared and scratched up, not fit for a gilded frame or a prominent shelf. As a trophy it would belie the scourge of his ripping flesh; his smile would twist into the maddening pain of his slow death ordeal. No, I don't think that I'll ever put up his picture. Regardless, I'll always cherish it and the thought that he must have been brave in those last hours. Brave but not a hero. Heroes are too hard to define, if they exist at all. None of us were heroes. We just did it, whatever it was, whatever it took to accomplish the mission, to live through it and to help others do the same to get back home.

Home, the way it was, to be boys again in the reassuring warmth and safety of the after glow of the 50s and early 60s. Boys, dreaming of their bull-nosed Chevys, drag racing down dark country roads after the football games. We had no clue that Ozzie and Harriet got lost in the shuffle. In the stupor of what was left of our youth, we could still numb the horror of the war by daydreaming of home, the way it was. We each had one special buddy that was our lifeline back to the world.

Bruce Howard Baumgarner, a PFC from California, was a nonstop daydream of home to me. Being in Delta Company, we only got together when our respective units came into base camp from the field. The occasional mortar attacks, in Cu Chi, were merely disturbances that had to be tolerated. We shared our innermost thoughts like brothers; all those stories of our girls, our cars and our lives back home. After a while, sitting in the Service Club, it was almost like being home in a bar.

So, when I left country two weeks before him, he died.

SSG Willie Tate told me that Bum spent the better part of a night bleeding to death in some shit hole corner of the Boi Loi Woods. As it started to get dark, a sniper took him down blowing off part of his left shoulder. They screamed for a medic, but when someone tried to reach him, the sniper shot the would be rescuer between the eyes. For the rest of the night they could hear him, but couldn't reach him. Where was his mind as he cried and bled in the darkness? What were his thoughts before he finally fell silent as dawn approached and all of his blood soaking into the thirsty jungle floor, our guys pinned down around him? Was he thinking of home? Was he holding on to the thought of meeting me at Christmas in San Francisco or was he imagining me, calling his house, asking to speak to him, and his father sobbing on the phone? What was he thinking in those long hours of torturous pain?

Thinking of him, I can smell the rotting jungle vegetation in my nostrils. I can feel that cold, damp dew all over me. I can just barely make out the limp, useless arm still attached, lying next to him in the moon lit clearing. I can feel from the essence of my soul, the deep truth within my heart that had I been there; he would have lived or I, also, would have died.

For the rest of my life, I'll be crawling through that thicket, trying to reach him.

Bruce Howard Baumgarner was KIA December 15, 1967. He was from Vallejo, California. His name is on the wall with over 58,000 other of his brothers.

The following is Matthews's thoughts and he follows with a poem he wrote and sent to me.

Thanks to Merrill and Gerald for helping me put a face on a place that I've only seen in my mind for all these years. It is one of those things that you're not sure if it really happened. In time, your mind fills with doubt as to whether it really took place. It gets stored in a quiet little corner of your head and starts to deteriorate. It just becomes a hurtful thing you instinctively know is taboo and is not to be brought up....

Then something happens to jar it loose. Your wife takes you to a Vietnam movie or someone starts taking about it at a reunion or you come across your award letter with that date on it or you see it in the social media... and there it is... the two men dying in your arms... back at the forefront of your thoughts... in living color... the stare of a thousand miles, the scare of a thousand life-times, coming at you, out of the darkness, straight across a Tay Nihn rice patty... the unbreakable bond between the living and the dead...It's all good because your brothers are there... a day in the life of an old Wolfhound... I'll shut up now, but I'll leave you with a little Wolfhound poem:

HERO

AND AS THE SUN SETS,
THE HERO COMES HOME,
ALWAYS UNCERTAIN,
ALWAYS ALONE.

HE WEARS ON HIS CHEST,
THE MEDALS OF OLD,
BUT KEEPS IN HIS HEART,
THE WOUND EVER COLD.

HE CARRIES IT WITH HIM,
ALONE IN HIS BED,
BUT DREAMS OF AN ANGEL,
TO WARD OFF THE DEAD.

AND AS THE DAWN BREAKS,
HE'LL NO LONGER ARISE,
AND THE PAIN OF THE WARRIOR,
WILL PASS FROM HIS EYES.

Matt Kritzer

Sergeant Cary Clark, Arkansas

One of my Sergeants from Vietnam lives in a town close to Little Rock, AR. He called me Christmas Eve of 2007 to tell me he had read "See The Dragon" and really enjoyed it. I said that I was ready and for him to let me have it with the mistakes he had found in the book. He told me that he thought it was "right on" and thanked me for it. I have talked to him three or four times

now and I am always impressed with how his memory is so sharp after 40 some years. I guess I didn't realize that our cadre were people too and really knew "their" people and cared. I think what amazes me the most is the details and names of men that were under him that he recalls. We talked about my friend Charlie Crowe (KIA Vietnam) for a while and he said one of the main reasons he was so sad that he had to miss the Lexington reunion was that he missed meeting some of Charlie's family that had gathered there.

Chuck Dean: A Co 2/27, California Boy

Chuck Dean is a guy that served the same time as I and has one of those great humors that so many of us were treated with almost on a daily basis.

Wolfhound Story: *"Bruno Heel"*

October 1966 (I think).

Hobo, Bolai, VN or one of those places that nightmares were made of.

We had been dropped off by chopper, and proceeded with our Search and Destroy. We made some find, enough so that we were alerted that we were to make preparations for an extended stay. We grouped and formed a perimeter. Choppers were called to send out Sand Bags, and that's when we realized that we were going to occupy this piece of real estate for some time. The bunker that I was assigned to was to be the .50 cal bunker. My first thoughts were, "Great that means the fire will be concentrated on our location." Robert Taylor, my squad leader, and another guy were to be manning the gun.

While we were filling sand bags the bunker on the left was being manned by a Dog Handler from the 38th Scout Dog platoon that was attached to HHC of the 2/27, and another A Company GI. The handler's dog was tied to a bunch of bamboo which made up the area to our rear. We had to make sure all of our bunker was "two bags thick." Needless to say it took us longer to build our fortifications than the rest of the guys. We all ate chow sitting on our bunkers while scanning the local horizon for activity.

When night fall came it wasn't long before Charley started to prep the area with sniper fire trying to harass us. Then the mortars started to fall and every one scrambled for cover. Our own weapon personnel started dropping flares into the area so we could see what was going on. I was hanging over the gun and concentrated on the area in front of the bunker. Taylor was on my left, and the other guy was on my right. I felt something on my neck, and I glanced slightly to my left and said, "Get your hairy arm off my neck."

Without hesitation Taylor said, "I don't have my arm around your neck and it isn't hairy anyway."

I glanced to my right and said, "Get your hairy arm off my neck," at which time his reply was, "My arm isn't hairy and it isn't around your neck anyway."

My first thought was, we are not alone in here. I reached back and felt a bunch of fur, and the angry, deep-throated growl of something.... Needless to say we all bailed out of the bunker and stood there. "What the hell is in the bunker?"

"I don't know, you go look see."

"No F...ing way am I going back into that bunker."

Well about this time the area in front of our bunker was being lit up like someone had lit off a Roman candle. The damn fire was hitting all around us and all we could do was argue about what was in our bunker. The firing quit after a while, and as it did, the Dog Handler yelled, "Bruno Heel!" Out of the bunker lunged this 100+ pound German Shepherd. All three of us looked at the dog and started to laugh. This was to be a moment we would never forget. Back in Cu Chi someone would yell "Bruno Heel" and we would laugh. This has been a private moment since leaving VN except I did tell it once before while swapping Wolfhound Stories Earlier this year in Columbia, SC.

Chuck Dean 3-25-2012

K-9

Tim Hummel with his dog Caleb

*Tim Hummel from Butler, Missouri was a dog handler in Vietnam during 1971 and 72. He tells me lots of "dog" stories and most of them are fairly humorous. As the previous story reflects well, you never can be too sure of what they will do next. Tim tells me that dogs make mistakes and do really stupid stuff sometimes. In Vietnam when handlers witnessed one of those acts from another handler's dog, they would exclaim "That sh*t runs down the leash!"*

Don't you just love the humor and wit of 20-year-olds?

Arthur Montgomery: Alone I Remain

The following is a short statement, but one that aptly describes the feelings of many who served. We all wonder.... This from Art. How sad.

I always wondered why I am now the only remaining member of my platoon alive. Most of them were killed in battle. A few were wounded and got state side. Mine were only scrapes in comparison. I never got Purple Heart for these as the medics took care of me just fine. The purple hearts belong to the ones more seriously wounded. Today I can't prove I was ever wounded. At my age now it doesn't mean a thing. I still remember everyone in my squad, and platoon. May they rest in peace.

ART

Dana "Shammer" Martin: Did We Change So Fast?

If you talk to any family member or friends of a soldier back from Vietnam, they will tell you of the striking change. Most of us felt the change coming over us at the time. It wasn't a good change, but maybe a necessary one. Maybe without that change survival would have been impossible. This next Wolfhound tells a short story about how fast he knew the "change" was upon him. He is Shammer.

1969 bunker story

We are getting older but still remember shit. Things that never go away. I got to FSB JACKSON on the afternoon of July 4th 1969. To be honest I didn't remember till later what day it was. That night we got mortared. George Johnson and I were huddled together trying to sleep. We were new and had no poncho liner.

Earlier in the evening we had ask one of the old guys where to sleep. He said take your pick; top of the bunker or in it. But the bunker has water in it. He asked us where our poncho liners were. We didn't know what the hell those were; he said they were like a blanket that even wet kept you warm. I asked him how to get one; he said the best way was to grab someone's who had been killed. This guy had stepped on 3 booby traps and was still in the field, and when he said that, he was so serious it shocked me.

Yeah things happen. When we got mortared one man died and one was blinded. George and I weren't really sleeping very well anyway so it seemed prudent to dive into the bunker full of water. I went out into the wire later to pull the blasting caps out of the claymores so the Dust Off could land. Shortly after returning inside the wire I ask that old timer if the man who died had a poncho liner. He said; yeah but it's already taken. Could I really get that way so fast?

Bob Park, Oregon: His List of Brothers Lost

The following is communications from Bob Park to me in late 2011. It is a few of his personal feelings and it is very emotional to read. I asked Bob if I could use it and he agreed. I believe he explains very well what thoughts stubbornly linger in the minds of those that were caught up in this terrible conflict. He includes three stories that are very typical of what most Vietnam veterans felt and endured. They laughed and they cried and they prayed and they joked and they got mad and they took care of each other.

The Roy (KIA November 5th 1966) Bob writes about is Roy Blewett from Iowa. Roy was one of my friends that I wrote about in See the Dragon.

It is sometimes easier to honor our friends as a group, but these were men with families and loved ones. Some hadn't even started to shave regularly, and really didn't know a lot about life. And remember the medics that purposely put themselves in harm's way to help the rest of us.

I had been keeping a small notebook since early Feb. 66 of those we had lost in A Co. 2/27. I felt it was important that these brothers would not be forgotten. This was long before there was even an idea of a "Wall." I had also added my own name on the last page just in case. As I thought of things or heard others mention these fallen, I would add comments and thoughts about them – it helped to keep their memory alive for me. As the year progressed, I also added the names of some men from other Companies that I had met or knew.

The following are the names I have in my notebook for November 5th, 1966. I know there were many more losses, especially from C/2/27 and A/1/27 not listed here, but these are the ones that I had met and knew.

Fred Mullen – Medic from HHC – he had been with us less than 2 months

Roy Blewett

John Caniff – Medic from HHC – He had arrived in March as a replacement

William "Buddy" Denman – He arrived the end of July as a replacement – My "little brother"

Lex Elswick

Lynn Russell – One of our original replacements that arrived the end of Feb. after Operation Circle Pines

Earl Hutton – He arrived the end of July as a replacement

Harry Lund – Medic from HHC and A Co

1LT Alan Perrault – He was only with us 11 days

Richard Spangler – Medic HHC & A Co

George "Gerry" Stoll

Bob Taylor

Luis Torres

Artie Walker

Bob Vest – He was with us less than two months

Gene Winters

James "Jimmy" Wright – He was C/2/27. He had just turned 18 in January and came in as a replacement the last week of May, 1966. He left a young wife.

There were also many wounded (including myself) – a few died of those wounds. Several were even given medals. Please give these warrior brothers the respect and honor they are due as individuals. They sacrificed even more than we did.

I was born and grew up in Portland, Oregon, and moved to Helix, Oregon when I retired from teaching in 2005. It is a very small town (180 pop) out in the middle of the wheat fields of North Eastern Oregon. I arrived in Vietnam in January 1966 – still feeling green and unsure of what was to come and a bit scared at times.

The 14th of February lost its charm for me in Vietnam. We were involved in Operation Taro Leaf and it was the first heavy fighting I was involved in. That was the day we lost our medics, too. Garry Coyle and Bob "Wrench" Roentsch. Technically they were from HHC, but they were with us. They even sent another medic from B Co. (Quick, I think) who was on our left flank to help Garry, but it was too late. Garry had been hit several times and when Quick got to him he was gone. Quick continued to help our men.

When SSG Duran, Cordie Dixon (a newbie only with us 7 days) and I started to move up to provide cover the Sergeant and then Cordie both went down. I was hit by a grazing bullet on the left arm, but didn't really notice it at the time. I was too busy trying to keep Cordie alive, which I failed to do. Wrench had been hit bad, but was still alive, so that just left Quick to tend the wounded. If my notes are right, Garry Coyle and Quick both received the DSC and Wrench got a Bronze Star. Wrench had died a few days later. SSG Duran and PFC Cordie Dixon only got Purple Hearts.

It was a terrible rude awakening for me. To see an 18-year-old kid and a 37-year-old Sergeant with a family so readily give up their lives to try and save their BIA (Brothers In Arms). They were the reason that I started keeping my diary of those that I knew who had been KIA. It was very important that their sacrifice not be forgotten. Before that day I had the feeling I was just an observer going through motions. Now the war was real. That was the first time I really cried in Vietnam.

The following are two letters I received from Bob Park in early November, 2011.

Don, It is a little after 5:00 AM my time this morning (Nov 4), and I have been awake almost an hour already. Today and tomorrow will be tough days for me. It was also a Friday 45 years ago today that we lost Col. Barott and your friend "Gater" was killed. I have him in my notebook as being a Sgt in C Co. Is that correct? I must have met him at some point, but am not sure when. I didn't know many people in C Co., but I know they took quite a few losses on the 4th including their Captain and a Lt. I do remember their medic, Rod Althoff who was also killed that day.

Tomorrow, the 5th is the worst for me as I lost some friends as well as being wounded myself. You mentioned Roy Blewett and another one for me was William "Buddy" Denman. He was one of our replacements that came the end of July. He was only 19 when he arrived. We celebrated our birthdays in August, mine on the 21st and his on the 25th. He was killed moving off the same hot LZ as Roy. We (A Co) lost several that day, too. I was wounded later on the 5th and didn't know about Buddy or Roy until I was brought back and I asked about them. Buddy was the toughest one for me to take as I had let him past the armor I had built up to protect myself. He was the same age as my younger brother would have been and even looked a bit like him. I tried to clue him in as to how to take care of himself, but I guess I didn't do my job too well. That was probably the first time I had really cried in several months.

I know from your book that you lost friends then also. SO – here is to our friends – They were Wolfhounds and our brothers in arms and well as in our hearts – they rest in good company.

Bob Park, Oregon

Don,

You are absolutely right, and I totally understand your feelings! I agree with your wanting the memories not to fade. When I first started keeping my notebook it was for just that reason. I never dreamed at that time there would ever be a "Wall," and even though the Wall does now exist, it is just a list of names; it doesn't speak about those people on it. It is left to us – the ones who knew them to add their humanity. They were people with families and friends, wives and lovers, and futures unfulfilled. They sacrificed too much, but in doing so, they made it possible for others like you and I to come back.

As I mentioned before, I never expected to come back myself. And to be perfectly honest, I didn't really think I had anything to come back to. It was people like Keith Kauffman and Carlos Sanchez and later, Harry Lund and John Caniff – all medics that patched me up, and SGT Gerry Stoll that kept ragging on me to be careful and help the new guys stay alive. They are all on the wall and here I am writing about them.

I also had two cousins and a best friend that were in Vietnam. One cousin, Walt Smith was in the Air Force and was already there when I went. We were the same age. He came home OK. The other was Robert Lee Park, (I am Robert James Park). He went into the Army in 1968. I was already out and finishing my college work. He called me when he finished his medic training and asked me about Vietnam. He knew he was going there, and was assigned to the 5th Cav, 9th Inf Div. I told him some things about the country, and how important the medics were and that his fellow soldier's lives would depend on him doing the best job he could for them. I didn't have the heart to tell him how many medics we had lost. He went in country in March, 1969 and was KIA 18 Apr 1969. He left a new wife (Sherri) and parents that never did fully recover.

One of my good friends was Kenny Alfstad. He went into the Army shortly after I did and was also at Ft Ord for basic. He decided to go Airborne so he arrived in Vietnam the first week of July , 1966 and was assigned to B Company, 2nd Bn, 327th Infantry of the 101st Airborne ABN Division. We were going to try to get together on R&R, but he was KIA on 3 Oct, 1966, 3 weeks short of his 20th birthday.

Such a waste!

Story 1

In May, 1966 during the last part of the month I think, we had some down time and I was assigned to "burn the shit." Those fantastic Latrines we had always made me think of long underwear with the trap door seats in the back. You had to open the back trap door and pull the drums out to burn them. And what a lovely aroma, the fuel just helped to enhance the odor. Some guy from the 1/27 came over and said he had lost a couple rifle rounds "down the hole" while sitting and loading a clip, and wanted me to be careful and maybe try and find them before I set the tub on fire. He said he didn't want me to get hurt if one of them exploded because of the heat. I, in my innocence, thought he was being very serious, and decided I had best shovel the shit out into another drum and see if I could find the shells. Of course there were no lost rounds, and they had a good laugh at my expense while I was getting dirty and stinky shoveling shit. I of course had my revenge. I figured the burning sack of shit on the door step would be too obvious, so I got a bucket and put some "latrine matter" in it, and while that particular platoon was out, I spread the "matter" all over the ground at the front entrance of their hooch. I didn't think that was too bad for a city kid that spent his summers on a farm cleaning out barns and pigpens.

Story 2

In March, 1966 we were on an S&D sweep SW of Cu Chi and were moving westward along a small river (name unknown). We had stopped for a short break and an old-timer named Sands (Sp4 Okey Sands) decided he needed to take a shit. He walked out in the river to about his knees, squatted slightly, and dropped the back of his pants and proceeded to relieve himself. You could hear the splash and then he started yelling and trying to get back up on the shore with his pants still half down. We started cracking up and laughing so hard that the tears started running down my face. He had been standing in kind of an eddy in the river and the package he had left was swirling around and trying to get back to him and he was running from it. We all generated a few jokes about that at Okey's expense. We had all been rather tense and it was a great pressure release.

Okey was from a small town called Nutter Fort outside of Clarksburg, WV. He was what I would call a true hillbilly. He was the nicest guy and would do anything to help you. He was older than most of us (he was 27 and I was 22 at that time), and I think, he had come from Hawaii with the rest of us. I didn't get to know him until after I arrived in mid January, 1966. Okey, along with two other guys (Walt Anderson and Mike McGoldrick) were killed 16 April 66. They were listed as "Non Hostile Accident" casualties. I never considered Mortars "non-hostile".

Story 3

This is about PFC William Luther "Buddy" Denman. I had mentioned him to you before; this is just a bit more detailed.

When Buddy arrived the last week of July, 1966 I really did a double take. He was 19 and the spitting image of my younger brother who would have also been 19, but had been killed in an auto accident a few years before. Buddy was assigned to 1st platoon, A Co (I was in 3rd platoon). We were preparing to join Operation Koko Head in progress so he was thrown into the action right away. I didn't really see him enough to talk with him again until we got back to base on 4 August, 1966. I made it a point to introduce myself to him, I asked if he wanted to be called William or Bill and he told me, "It doesn't matter, but my friends call me Buddy." I told him, "Then Buddy it is! We are all friends and brothers here. We all watch out for each other. My name is Robert or Bob, but some call me Bear."

That was how it started for us. I welcomed him to the Wolfhounds. He had already met his platoon and I introduced him around to people I knew. Buddy was independent and didn't expect anything special for himself. He wanted to fit in and be another one of the guys.

He had a hard life as a kid, but always had a smile when he talked with you. He had a girlfriend named Pat that he was planning on marrying when he got back. He seemed to really like the Army, but I was never sure he could handle the job he had. Buddy had tried to get in the Marines, but they wouldn't take him so he came to the Army. At that time, the Army would take anyone who could see lightning and hear thunder, so he made it in.

First platoon had Mike Marcukaitis who had arrived about two or three weeks before Buddy, Lynn Russell, Bruce Manual, Verdell Hildreth and Jim Glasgow to name a few, and Buddy seemed to fit right in. He and Rodney Wapoose also hit it off pretty well.

We had lost Jose Rivera, Alton Price, and Danny Roeckl during Koko Head and Mike Marcukaitis had been wounded along with some others. I think that was Buddy's first taste of having brother soldiers wounded or killed. I tried to talk with Buddy about what he had been through after the operation, but he wasn't very talkative then. Later he did open up some. One of the things I noticed with Buddy was his eyes. They say the eyes are the window to the soul, and Buddy seemed to have sad eyes. Later, as he slowly told me more about his earlier life, I could better understand why. But for now, all he had mentioned was his mother and sister and just said his dad had died when he was a kid. He always liked talking about his girlfriend Pat.

It was really nice to be at base camp and eating real food (instead of "C" rations) when our birthdays rolled around. I had received a big care package from my parents, and of course you always shared it with your brothers. My birthday was August 21st and Buddy's was August 25th so I made sure he got a bunch of the stuff. We even ate the stale popcorn the goodies were packed in. Buddy had turned 20 and I had turned 23. The one sad note was that Jose (Rivera) was supposed to have celebrated with us too. He would have had his 21st birthday on August 16th.

I don't know if Buddy ever mentioned in his letters home about what he had to do, but none of it was very pleasant. It was monsoon season and we were always wet. It was better if you didn't wear underwear, because you would develop some nasty fungal infections if you did for very long and were continually soaked. That included your feet and other parts of your body. You had to learn to sleep in short spurts and someone always had to be awake – especially if you were at a LP (Listening Post) or in the field very long. The mosquitoes and leaches were another problem. Bombshell Crater baths were common. You could wash your clothes and yourself at the same time. If you wore socks (which I had to, to prevent blisters), you took them off at night and wrung them out and let them dry. I had seen sox actually pull off in pieces because they had rotted in your boots. We would be soaked with rain and the sun would suddenly come out and you could see the steam rising off the uniforms as they quickly dried. Then it was just the sweat that kept you wet until the next downpour. The heat was oppressive – especially with the high humidity.

The monsoon season ended the first part of October, and then it was just the heat as everything dried out.

I don't think I ever heard Buddy seriously complain. We all had our little gripes, but Buddy would put up with all the Shit we had to do and he would always do a good job, even when he was literally burning the Shit from the latrines. He learned quickly and didn't make the same mistake more than once. He also learned to ask if he was not sure. He did miss his family and his girlfriend, but he had also found a home in the Army, at least for a while. He seemed to really like it.

With Buddy it was the little things, like his smile, or when he would pat me on the back and say. "Thanks Bear" (my nickname). He wasn't above playing a joke on someone, but it was never malicious or hurtful. I don't remember ever seeing Buddy mad or angry (except maybe at himself).

We had another Operation (Sunset Beach) the 2nd week of September that kept us out for about 10 days. If I remember right, as soon as Buddy got back, he was given guard duty. He fell asleep and got an ass chewing and maybe lost a stripe over that. We had two more search and destroys the end of September and the second week of October. Buddy was learning and getting the routine down and doing a good job. If anything he was becoming a bit too "Gung Ho" and maybe taking unnecessary chances. I had to pull him back once because he almost tripped a booby trap.

Buddy had a heart of gold, but didn't mind pulling a prank on someone else. He told me about his raising sheep when he was in High School for the 4-H or FFA (I'm not sure which.) I used to give him a ba-a-ad time about that - asking him if he had any special favorites, or if his girlfriend Pat minded (A farm boy Joke).

I guess I got to know Buddy because he was so much like my brother, even in his actions. But he was also his own person. He was a terrific young man just moving into adulthood, it was obvious that he had not had an easy childhood but he had been fortunate in having friends and a second family to support and help him through the rough times.

Buddy was killed on November 5th, 1966. We lost a lot of good people that day. People like Aaron Thomas, Roy Blewett, Les Elswick, Lynn Russell, and a young 18 year old medic named Harry Lund. He had been with us since right after Operation Taro Leaf in February. He had patched me up a couple times. He had been so nervous during Circle Pines (April 5th), that he was shaking while he was trying to get a bandage on my wound. I kept talking to him – asking where he was from and what he wanted to do when he got back to the real world – It helped calm him down. It turned out he was from Chehalis, Washington – just a short run up the freeway from Portland, Oregon – my home town. After that, we often talked about getting together again after we were home.

There were many others also KIA that day and even more wounded including myself. It was a time when ordinary men were asked to do extraordinary deeds. It was called Operation Attleboro. There were a lot of medals given out after that action, both to the living and the dead.

I didn't find out until I was back at the Evac Hospital about Buddy. He had been one of the first ones KIA at the Hot LZ along with Harry and Lynn. Others like Roy and Aaron were KIA while trying to save others.

I knew Buddy wasn't a replacement for my real brother, but he was my Brother in Arms, and he was one of the few people I had let in passed the wall I had built to protect myself from being hurt, so when I found out he had been killed, it was a very hard time for me.

I wished it had been me – not him. I had already lost too much and had nothing to go back to the real world for. Buddy was so young and had friends and family waiting for him along with his girlfriend. That was the second and last time I really broke down and cried while in Vietnam. It was such a terrible waste – all those young men.

Mike Cassidy, Myrtle Point, Florida

Mike Cassidy served with the First Battalion (The sister to the 2nd Bat) of Wolfhounds. So not working with him, I never knew him until 45 years after we came home. He is a great guy and a guy that loves to talk about his long term marriage (41years) to the love of his life and his many fishing trips. Mike is fun to talk to and a real pleasure to know.

Mike tells me this picture was taken right after being thrown in the mud hole behind the Alpha Co 1st Sgt's hooch. The traditional act when a man was promoted, to Spec 4 in his case.

"Warrior 33, this is Mustang 33"

Paul Mehl and I were both in 1/27 A first platoon. I was offered a job working in 2nd Brigade operations in the Tactical Operations Center and was working there and Paul got out of the field due to a fungus on his body that the medics couldn't get rid of. He had the same job as me only he worked in the 1/27 TOC. We relayed messages, kept maps posted and current, cleared H and I artillery sites, ordered dustoffs and anything else relating to operations.

The First Hounds did a combat assault to the Northwest of Saigon and West of Hoc Mon in a swampy area. They hit the jackpot and found a NVA rest camp, there were at least a couple of companies there having a R and R. They didn't have any defense together and the Hounds swept through amassing a big body count and taking POWs with almost no friendly casualties.

The reports from the field would go to Paul and he would relay them to brigade. Since we were friends and knew what we could get away with it, Paul would radio me with a body count and I would add a 1 to the front of the number or just add several to the body count.

A typical radio exchange would go something like this:

Paul: "Warrior 33, this is Mustang 33"

I would answer and Paul would know my voice.

Paul: "Warrior 33, Mustang Alpha has a body count of 5 at X-ray Tango123456 (location on map)."

Me: "Mustang 33 roger, understand bravo charlie of one five."

Paul: (long pause) "Ahhhh, Warrior 33, that's affirmative one five."

We could do this because no one listened to the routine radio traffic, it was usually very boring. So this went on for several hours as the sweep progressed through the NVA base camp. After a while Paul would do his own padding of the body count and between us we must have added at least 50. I don't remember what the real count was but by the time Paul and I were done it was probably double. And since the information was in the logs for both battalion and brigade it was true.

Another quick story about 4th of July, 1968.

Brigade had set up a forward TOC in the engineer compound at Hoc Mon. The 4 companies of the 1/27 were in company sized base camps all along the Hoc Mon canal with one company on Hoc Mon bridge.

Major Bruce Smalley, the operations officer for the First Hounds, had come in to meet with the brigade operations officer to go over the next day's operations and he pulled me aside. He told me to watch the area where all the companies were just after dark. He didn't give a reason, just to look. So at the prescribed time I'm starring off into the dark and I think every man that wasn't out on ambush set off a star cluster or parachute flare. Best and most meaningful 4th of July fireworks I have ever seen.

The body count was a big deal to upper level staff. If you remember McNamara was trying to run a war by computer for the first time and body count was an important statistic to the men in power. In the brigade TOC we had a sign on the wall that listed the body counts for all three brigades. It was kept current by the S-2 staff and lord help them if it was a day behind. Didn't keep up on our own KIA/WIA numbers but the body count was of great interest.

Paul Mehl passed away a few years ago. We were the only ones that knew about our "conspiracy", it was just something that happened on the spur of the moment. If anyone knew about it our young asses would have been shipped back on line.

Sergeant Major Cobb: Two War Wolfhound

Colonel George Armstrong Custer III, the Commanding Officer and Command Sergeant Major Cobb of the 2/27, 1969

By Franz "Rosie" Rosina & Teddy Dave Hale

Ted and I were standing amongst a large group of Wolfhounds and their families waiting to have our picture taken at the Branson, Missouri Reunion. What happened next took me by total surprise.

I was handed a note from this elderly gentleman standing directly in front of me; the note read "I know you guys, David Cobb". I turned to Teddy in shock, as I said to Ted "Teddy this is

Sergeant Major Cobb!" The look on my partners face was beyond my ability to describe, after forty-one years we were once again united. CSM. David Cobb holds the Combat Infantryman's badge for action in three wars; he fought in Italy during WWII, Korea and Vietnam after which he then retired. There is another CSM in our organization who was a Three war Wolfhound and we salute him. Our reason however, for wanting to recognize David Cobb, is out of great admiration for him; he was many things to Teddy and me, he was a mentor to me and set an example for us to follow.

On February7, 1951 in one of the few bayonet charges in modern times, Captain Lewis Millet led the men of Easy Co. 2nd • Bn.2th Inf. Rgt. "Wolfhounds" to seize hill 180 in the vicinity of Som-NI Korea from the Chinese. One of the members present at the battle of Bayonet Hill as it is now known, was David Cobb. Teddy and I became familiar with CSM David Cobb during another war, "Vietnam." The year was 1969 he was Command Sergeant Major of the 2/27 under Colonel George Armstrong Custer III, who was the commanding officer. The AO's (Area of Operations) were many, Cu Chi, Jackson FSB, Dau Tieng, Kotric, the sugar mill, the Michelan Rubber Plantation, the Co Vom Dong River Operation, Phuc Lu Village, the list is endless. CSM Cobb tried to visit a patrol base every day. I had many experiences with the CSM, both in Delta Co. and as a member of the sniper team led by Sergeant Nelson Fox, but the story of the "Wolfhounds on Rat Patrol" written by Sergeant Teddy Hale is a story worth telling.

After hearing of the N.V.A. on Highway One from Fire Support Base Jackson to Cu Chi base camp, home of the 25th Inf. Div. "Topic Lightning" CSM. Cobb decided to form a "Rat Patrol" based on the television series about a British "Desert Rats" mobile jeep unit during WWII. Our mission was to investigate these rumors. At F.S.B. Jackson, CSM Cobb asked Rosina and me what we thought of the idea. We didn't like it, the thought of being guinea pigs riding up and down Highway One in jeeps getting shot at, was to say the least, not at all appealing. "Nec Aspera Terrent". After talking to the CSM, we decided to "Give it a Go." We rigged three jeeps with radios, M-60's on mounts, M-16's, M79's, Laws Flairs, grenades and anything else we thought we could use. We managed to talk four other fools into going with us.

The first night out we made the run back to Cu Chi. I was driving, the CSM was handling the Commo and "Rosie" manned the M-60 machine gun, we were pretty scared although we didn't see anything, the thought of riding around out there in jeeps was spooky. We were coming into a small village, when a large hog came running out from the left side of the jeep. Rosie and the other 60's opened fire and the hog was dead. Well needless to say a papa san came running up to us after we stopped, raising hell. CSM. Cobb calmed him down, reassuring him that he would be reimbursed for the hog; we continued on our way. The next day CSM Cobb returned to the village and made good his promise, he paid papa san twice the hog's value. Col. Custer didn't really like the idea of the "Rat Patrol" and didn't like the fact that we killed papa san's hog. CSM Cobb didn't even get a pork chop out of the deal.

After a week the CSM came to me and Rosie and said to get things ready. He told us to get volunteers to go back out that night, so Rosie and I started asking around Jackson and came up with seven men to man our three vehicles. Three drivers, three gunners and the CSM. We pulled out of Jackson around 2100 hrs. and drove for about two hours when all hell broke out, we were taking heavy small arms fire from the driver's side, the fire was coming from a hedgerow across a rice paddy. The sixties put out a good suppressive fire. The CSM Called for a marking round, he adjusted fire and the "ARTY" began to light up the sky. The 60's, 16's and "ARTY" went on for what seemed like 30 minutes when the CSM ordered cease fire.

All was calm, the crackling of the radio broke the silence. CSM Cobb reported to Col. Custer. Custer ordered us to sweep the area for a body count. After about 2 hours or more we had a total of three NVA bodies confirmed. Col. Custer thought the

"Rat Patrol" was a success and a good idea from then on. Our third "Rat Patrol", CSM Cobb came to me and said "Lets go out tonight, get the men together." I gathered up a crew of seven, we pulled out after 2100 hrs. it was a calm night, we were coming back in and had one round fired at us. We primped the area with M-60's and M-16's. CSM Cobb called in for artillery flairs from Jackson. We stopped firing, all was calm again, we held our A.A. and we requested parachute flares about every 10 to 15 minutes. After an hour we pulled out and headed back to Jackson.

This was my last "Rat Patrol," but all said and done, CSM Cobb was cool under fire, he was a "True Pro" there was no one ever hurt in any way on my three trips on "Rat Patrol." CSM David Cobb and his wife Ann attended the Branson, Missouri and Colorado Springs reunion. We hope to be reunited with him at the Baltimore reunion. Until then, God Bless.

Franz "Rosie" Rosina, USA Ret.

Guy Hinton, Cincinnati, Ohio: Small World!

This photo was taken sometime in November 1968 by my friend Gilbert Calaf who passed away in October 2010. We were on a convoy headed back to Tay Ninh province from the Cu Chi area.

We were going back to the area where our platoon was nearly overrun by battalion of NVA on August 20, 1968. Paul Lambers won the MOH in that battle. I was still scared from the experience. I think Gilbert really captured it in the photo. We also spent the latter part of August and most of September fighting the NVA in the Tay Ninh province. --Guy Hinton

Guy Hinton is absolutely one of my all-time favorite people. Extremely funny guy, but a very dry sense of humor. One of those guys you have to pay attention to or you'll miss something really good.

Guy and wife Sylvia along with about 150 Wolfhounds had been several days reunionizing in Branson, Missouri. Many of us departed the reunion the same morning including the Hintons and

Sue and I. I got a call from Guy about the time we got back home. He said, "I bet I had a more exciting trip home than you." Turns out that he did. This is how Guy described the one in a million encounter.

The buddy that I met in Branson, Missouri was in the Walgreen's parking lot. He was on a motorcycle. Sylvia and I struck up a conversation with him and his wife. Before I went into the store, I warned them that Sylvia would talk their ears off. When I came out of the store, Sylvia was still talking to them. She told me that he was with the Wolfhounds. So I asked his name. He said it was Don Pitkin. I told him that I knew him. I was with him the night we were mortared by our own four deuce mortars in Tayninh province. I called in his dust off and helped load him on the medevac. I mentioned him in the November section of my story.

Here is Guy to describe his tour in Vietnam in his words.

I graduated from the University of Cincinnati Magna Cum Laude in 1974. I learned a lot in school. However, my Vietnam tour from June 1968 to June 1969 was greatest learning experience of my adult life. Some lessons were hard to take but I feel that I am a better man for having had them.

Everyone who did a tour has their own perspective on what it did to or for them. Although you were with brothers in arms, in reality you were alone in enduring and processing the experiences in your mind.

My tour was probably like countless others. I remember sights, smells, sounds, names, faces, dates, terror, boredom, guilt, anger and joy. My MOS was 11B.

June

When the plane approached Ton Son Nhut air base, I was expecting to see mortar and machine gun fire greeting us upon landing. Instead we landed upon a quiet and bumpy runway. As the doors were opened I remember the humidity and smell that intruded upon the cabin. I still chuckle about MPs boarding the plane to ask if anyone had any porn or drugs to surrender.

I knew they weren't talking to me. My drug experience had only been aspirin for headaches, cough syrup for colds and tincture of iodine for cuts and scrapes.

My first in country meal was salisbury steak, mashed potatoes with gravy, green beans, and a freshly baked roll. It was memorable. As we moved through the chow line, the monsoon winds and rains started up. The rain came in torrents. The wind blew it through the mess hall. My steak, potatoes, and green beans were soup. At least my fresh roll wasn't under water. I was looking forward to enjoying it, until the big green blowfly crawled out from under and perched on top.

After three days at the replacement depot, unit assignments came down. I didn't know much about the Twenty Fifth Infantry Division. Although the electric strawberry patch was very colorful, I was a bit concerned about assignment to the Wolfhounds. The cadre at Long Binh would just refer to the Wolfhounds as some crazy Motherf*****s!

July

When I got to Cu Chi, I was assigned to Company A, 2nd Bn, 27th Infantry Regiment, Wolfhounds. This was my new home and identity. The Company was in for a stand down. I received what I guessed was the traditional FNG welcome. I was coated with shaving cream and unceremoniously tossed into an open sided utility trailer filled with beer, sodas, and ice!

I was assigned to the third platoon, commonly referred to as the third herd. The herd was quite a cross section of the American population. We had enlistees, draftees, jocks, colored guys and red necks from the rural south, farm boys from the mid west and Puerto Ricans from New York. We had dopers and boozers. We also had the bewildered (me).

I'll never forget that I smoked my first cigarette while a member of the herd. It was dusk and we were sweeping a village near Trang Bang. The VC cut loose with a barrage of auto weapons fire and pinned us down behind a paddy dike. This was the first time that anyone had shot at me. I was really scared and it showed. Gilbert Calaf, who became my best friend in Nam, offered me a Kent cigarette with a micronite filter to calm my jangled nerves. As we hunkered down, he said that the VC were just harassing us and would soon stop and run. He was right. They shot up their ammo and melted away to wherever VC melt away. Larry Tillman from Chicago was wounded in the leg and dusted off. He later came back to the field.

August

August started out uneventful. We did so many eagle flights and sweeps that I couldn't keep track of them. It seems that we traveled from one end of Tayninh province to the other and back again. The weather was sweltering. It was really a relief when the monsoon rains rolled in and cooled things off for the day.

I pulled my first overnight LP that month. I was really scared to be outside the perimeter at night. We set up by a water filled laterite pit. Rain poured and the wind howled all night. Even with a starlight scope, visibility was nil. Hearing was about the only sense that was not affected by the weather. I listened intently for the sounds of an enemy approach. All night we heard footsteps, but couldn't see any one. When dawn arrived, we learned the source of the footsteps. It was the wind blowing the laterite pit's water against the shoreline!

We humped as a company sized unit by day. We chased intel's leads on where we might make contact with the enemy. After humping all day, we set up platoon size perimeters, and tried to relax before dark. One of the things I enjoyed was reading and translating letters for my Puerto Rican friend, Gilbert (from the Bronx) who could speak but not read Spanish. I translated the letters written to him in Spanish into English. Then I wrote back to his girl friends in my best high school Spanish.

Everything was pretty much routine until about 1am on August 20th. That night permanently changed my view of the world. We were taking turns on watch. Our squad leader awakened us, and said, "They're here!" At first I didn't know who or how many were here. When the AKs, machine guns and RPGs started, I knew there were a lot more than I ever imagined. We were definitely outnumbered. Bobby Byrd next to me took a round in the back of his head right away. They got close enough to trade grenades with us. I must have thrown a dozen grenades to take out a machine gun that set up in front of our foxhole. I threw. They fired. I threw. They fired. I kept it up until they finally stopped.

We were in way over our heads. And were running low on ammo to boot. Our only choice was to fight and die or fight and live. The platoon leader was wounded in the head. Paul Lambers took over and was able to coordinate the air support for our tenuous position. We had illumination and mini-gun support from Spooky for several hours. As the NVA tightened the noose around us, it became necessary to walk the fire closer to our positions. The helicopter gunships needed to be able to determine exactly where our positions were located. We had no strobe lights, so we had to burn our clothing to mark our positions. The fire was walked so close that Greg Carr in our foxhole received a fatal head wound from a gunship rocket. When daylight arrived the enemy fled. We had several wounded that were dusted off. Our KIA were Bobby Byrd, Greg Carr, Ron Rummel, Fred Tappan, Jerry Sansing, Arcadio Torres, and Clifford Walker. The final enemy body count was 156. The brass came out for a photo opp.

Paul Lambers received the Medal of Honor for his actions. My good friends Ray Roiger and Ken Cobb received Silver Stars for their heroic actions that night. We were sent to Tayninh base camp to recover from the battle.

We must have recovered very fast. On August 24th, we were sent to fire base Schofield. The NVA attacked us our first night there. The body count was 62 enemy KIA. The worst part of this battle was searching bodies for info that that might be useful. After we searched bodies, we searched and cleared the bunkers and trenches of their base camp.

This was August. I only had 10 more months to go!

September

As far as wars go, September was a pretty decent month. We hadn't seen too much contact. The usual routine was helicopter here, there and everywhere. Sweep and cordon off villages. I remember being part of a blocking force at a village that was known to harbor the VC. It was very lush and green. Psychological operations flew choppers equipped with loud speakers over the village and dropped leaflets to warn the people to evacuate the village. They were warned that artillery would be fired on the village. I don't remember how many people fled the village. I do remember lying behind a paddy dike with Ray Roiger while the artillery flew overhead and slammed into the village. While lying there I heard something whizzing through the air. It was a piece of shrapnel. It hit me in the helmet and bounced onto Ray's back. When it landed on his back, it sizzled. It was hot and heavy. I still thank God for my steel pot. After the artillery had finished, we had to search the village. I spent most of that day in a big hut that was used to store rice. When we entered, there was a woman wailing in the corner. We weren't sure what she was doing there. So, we had the interpreter ask her. She pointed to smoldering stack of burlap rice bags. We moved the bags off of her daughter's body. I located a C ration box to hold the remains.

I scooped them up with an entrenching tool. The head was the last piece that I located. It rolled off the blade and when it hit the floor, it broke open like a huge egg.

The worst thing that happened that month was on the 23rd. We were setting up a company size perimeter next to an ARVN compound. The ARVN had told us where to set up. As we laid out our positions, JE Thompson and I were standing next to one another. We heard a popping sound, and JE grabbed my shoulder and made an awful moaning sound. We both looked down. His right foot was gone. It landed right in front of us. The ARVN had told us to set up in area that they had mined to protect their compound. I remember the last JE said to us as we loaded him on the chopper. He said, “Ain’t this a pisser?”

Only 9 more months to go!

October

This was a good month. Alpha Company had the opportunity to guard the Phu Cuong bridge over the river flowing to Saigon. The third platoon was guarding the bridge over the Ba Bep canal. We manned check points on each side of the road leading to the bridge. I was now the RTO for the third platoon. We had a bunker with electricity and cots. There was even a mess sergeant who cooked hot chow for us. The Phu Cuong bridge was about

1000 feet long. It cost approximately 2 million dollars and took several years to build. Unfortunately, the VC's sappers were able to blow it up in one night by floating explosives down river and attaching them to the piers. The cost to rebuild it was 10 million dollars.

I also had an opportunity to go on an ambush patrol with an American advisor and his ARVN platoon. That was first and last time that I would work with the locals. We moved out at dark. When we arrived and set up, I heard Vietnamese music, talking, and the hiss of soda cans being opened. It was the ARVN! I got the idea that they were alerting the VC to their presence. It was as if they were communicating, "You leave us alone and we'll leave you alone."

Only 8 months left !

November

We went back to Tayninh province this month. Based on my last visit, I was apprehensive that something bad was going to happen. We took a convoy to Tayninh base camp. I had heard a lot about convoys being ambushed and being pinned down on the open road. We made it to the base camp. From there we started chasing the NVA all over the province. Contact was sporadic. We conducted company size sweeps and set up overnight positions in the field.

Three events occurred that convinced me that my guardian angel was looking out for me. One night we were digging in for the night. I had dug a foxhole near a bamboo thicket. I thought that it would provide cover if we received fire from the rear. I had a strange feeling that the position was not right. If an RPG were to hit the bamboo, I would be cut up from the blast. So, I moved and dug another position. Don Pitkin, RTO for our artillery forward observer, moved into my vacated position. That night, we were mortared. Our four deuce mortars hit our location by mistake. Don was hit in the leg with shrapnel and dusted off. I never saw him again for 40 years when I ran into him and his wife in a parking lot in Branson, Missouri!

A few days later, we were sent out on a squad size ambush. We set up in a graveyard. The NVA hit the company perimeter and were rushing back to their own place of sanctuary. As luck would have it, their escape route was right through the grave yard. We could hear them chattering as they made directly for our position. My heart was pounding so hard that I thought they could hear it. We sprang the ambush with grenades then used our other weapons. At daybreak, we checked on their dead and wounded. There was a blood trail through the elephant grass. We followed it for about an hour before we gave up and returned to the ambush site. The enemy soldier we had been tracking had a machine gun and fired at the battalion CO's helicopter. We were chewed out for not finding the machine gunner. We were lucky. We could have walked into an ambush.

On November 27th we were set up along a canal somewhere along the Cambodian border. My R&R was coming up in December. I was sharing a fighting position with Dickie Devins and Carl Peters. As the light was failing, the last resupply chopper came. I was asked if I wanted to catch a lift to CuChi and get ready for R&R. I wasted no time getting my gear and my ass on that bird. Next morning, I was walking down the street in CuChi and saw Tim Petersman. I asked what he was doing in camp since the company was in the field. He told me that the perimeter had been hit last night and the gooks got through the wire. Dickie had been killed by an unexploded RPG in his chest. Carl had been shot in the leg and would probably lose it. I visited Carl in the hospital before I went to Hawaii for R&R to see my wife. Carl was heavily sedated all bandaged up. Seeing him that way made me ill. That could have been me. Carl died from his wounds in March 1969.

Only 7 more months to go!

December

Hawaii!! I met my wife Sylvia on R&R. We had three days and 4 nights to get reacquainted. We rented a Triumph 650 motorcycle to tour the Island. We had the wind in our faces and no cares for anything but each other. We were wined and dined by a congressional delegation on a fact finding tour about Vietnam. The food was great and drinks were plentiful. Maybe they were too plentiful. I didn't have any thing pleasant to say about my in country assignment. The time went so fast. It was difficult to say goodbye to my wife. We didn't know if we would ever see each other again. I can remember leaving on the bus to the airport from Fort Derussy. The bus had stopped at a light. Sylvia was standing there. She didn't see me watching her through the window. She was crying. I wanted to get off and hold her, but I couldn't. I wouldn't hold her again until June the following year.

While I was on R&R, someone must have said something good about me. When I got back, we were at FSB Jackson and had a new CO, Captain Clarence Cornett. I was no longer the third platoon RTO. I was going to carry the radio for the CO. It was a promotion that carried a lot more responsibility. I was ready for the change. I was now in the know about what was going on at the platoon, company and battalion levels. The job also had some perks which included no more perimeter guard, LPs or ambush patrols. I was also surrounded by a company of well-armed

Wolfhounds. My weapon was now my voice and ability to quickly interpret and accurately relay information.

We left FSB Jackson to establish a company perimeter west of TrangBang between a village and a huge marsh with lots of tall grass. It was the dry season and the sky was so clear and starry at night. I remember talking to our Vietnamese interpreter during the Apollo 10 mission. He couldn't believe that there were men orbiting the moon while we watched from the earth below. I remember wondering aloud, "If we can do something like that, why can't we figure out how settle our differences without killing one another?"

Some of the guys got to see the Bob Hope show in CuChi. I stayed in the field with the company. For Christmas, I got a great care package from my wife, home made cookies, summer sausage, crackers, nuts and a bottle of Sam Clay whiskey. The whiskey was a real surprise. It was from my father in law. He cut the bottoms out of two tomato juice cans, padded the sides of the bottle before putting it into the two cans. Once the bottle was inside, he soldered the cans together. We opened it with a P38 can opener. Everyone was surprised to be able to have a Christmas drink in the field. On Christmas eve, some troops at a not too distant firebase launched parachute flares in to the sky. They made the shape of a Christmas tree. It was really pretty to see a tree floating in the night sky.

Six more months to go!

January

We stayed in our hard spot and ran patrols into the village and the surrounding countryside. The village was called An Hoa. It seems that every day brought sniper fire and booby trap casualties. We had little luck in catching the perpetrators. They were really adept at harassing us and vanishing into their hidden tunnels. Sometimes we would get bored and look for something to entertain us. There was an old deserted house, probably built by the French. Although it was run down from years of neglect, it was pretty to look at from a distance. It had white stucco walls, a red tile roof, shutters and wooden floors. It had a great view of the tall grass of the marsh. It was used as an observation post. I wondered who might have lived there before it became a casualty of the changing times. If its walls could talk, what stories would they tell? Anyway let's get back to boredom. When no one was using it as an OP, we would use it for target practice with our LAWs (light anti tank weapons). At the time, it was fun. In retrospect, it was destructive.

I witnessed other behaviors that I had not expected to see. I watched the ARVN interrogate an enemy soldier. The soldier was tied up and lying on his back. They would punch him in the solar plexus to knock the wind out of him. When he gasped for breath, they poured whiskey down his nose and throat. They did this until they realized that he wouldn't talk. Their next strategy worked. They took a field telephone with a hand crank generator and attached it to his genitals. He wouldn't stop talking.

On another occasion, we accompanied the ARVN on an intel mission in the village. They had captured a VC who was supposed to be a colonel with extensive knowledge of the tunnel complex in the village. The prisoner led us around in circles for a couple of hours. He never willingly showed the tunnel locations. While walking ahead of the ARVN, he made a break for it. The ARVN shot him about three feet from a well. The tunnel he was headed for was just above the waterline inside the well. So, we found the tunnel and had to dispose of a dead VC body. We moved down the trail and waited for the ARVN to catch up. After about fifteen minutes, there was an explosion and red mist drifting through the air towards us.

Although it was a war, I do have recollections that make me smile in bewilderment. We had a shower. It was a big canvas bag suspended from a wood frame. The bag had to be filled by hand. So the idea was to use as little water as possible. You would lather up and rinse. One day the CO was all lathered up and had not yet rinsed when the VC crept up to a hedgerow and fired their AKs and machine guns. It was an incredible sight to see the CO all soaped up and low crawling through the dirt wearing only his steel pot. That was also the incident that caused the battalion CO to chew my ass. He was buzzing around in his helicopter when he heard the gunfire. I had the radio and I was ducking bullets. He had more questions than I had answers. I don't remember my exact words but they were to the effect, "I'll get the answers and call you back OUT!" He was livid. He got back on the horn and told me to never out him again.

I must have been pretty cocky. I had my 21st birthday in January and only had five more months to go!

February

VC control of the village was ended. Rome plows were unleashed on the village. I don't know where the people went. It was time to relocate to another perimeter up the road. Dismantling the bunker was quite memorable. Tearing the roof off was a hot and sweaty job. When we started tearing down the sidewall's sand bags, we learned that we were rooming with big black rats. We chased them with entrenching tools. Some were killed, and some got away without their tails.

Anyway, we moved a few clicks away to another hard spot. More sweeps and eagle flights to where I can't remember. In our new digs, we were mortared several times. Around February 14th I was hit by shrapnel above the right eye from one of the mortar explosions. However, the most memorable event for me was being stung by a scorpion in the dark. I went outside the bunker to get a soda from a metal ammo can. I was wearing flip flop sandals and the little black creature stung me on the right heel. It was the most pain that I had ever experienced in my tour.

The scorpion sting and the shrapnel made me start to think my luck might be running out. I was tired of the war and hoped to survive the next four months.

March

We moved again. In fact we moved so many times that I can't remember the names of the fire support bases that we populated. I remember mostly that they were hot dusty and devoid of vegetation.

The eagle flights continued without let up. It seems that we were just looking for trouble. As I recall, we found it on a riverbank on March 15th.

We had intel that the VC had a hospital somewhere in the area we were to be inserted in by chopper. We were warned that the LZ might be hot. As we approached, gun ships prepped the area with rockets, machine gun fire and a smoke screen to prevent the enemy from having a clear vision of our landing along the river bank. We landed without incident. As soon as the last troops departed the choppers, that was no longer the case. From the wood line, the machine guns and AKs started firing. As we hit the ground to survey our predicament, the mortars started to fall. We were pinned down in the open. The hedgerow that could provide cover was already occupied by the enemy. They were determined to keep us out! We also had sniper fire at our rear. We were being shot at from the other side of the river.

I had a new PRC77 radio with a whip antenna. I took a round through the speaker box. (It was like I was waving a sign that said shoot here for bonus points!) We called artillery support on the hedgerow. The artillery banged away. The small arms and mortars kept coming. We called in Cobra gun ships to work the hedgerow. When they went off station, the firing resumed. We were finally able to relay the gravity of our predicament. A napalm strike was made. I still remember the sight, sound, smell and heat of the strike. It was the only time that I saw first hand what napalm could accomplish. The firing stopped. We had one KIA, Sgt. Fred Brown, from the mortar fire. When the firing stopped, we were airlifted back to a fire support base. We never found out what was so important behind that hedgerow.

When we made it back, I was chewed by the first sergeant for not taking better care of the new PRC77 radio.

Although I had three months to go, I had more than enough excitement to last a lifetime.

April

Wrong!

Something out the ordinary was being undertaken. On April 5th we were sent to a barren spot in on the Cambodian border. Our mission was to build a fire support base from scratch in the hours from dawn to dusk. The base was to be called Diamond II. It was named after an earlier base that had been set up in February, and attacked by the NVA.

Most of the firebases I had helped to build were pretty simply dug by hand. Dig fighting positions. Fill sandbags. String concertina wire. Watch for enemy while the artillery positions were built. This base was different. Bulldozers were flown in to shape the terrain and build berms around the perimeter of the base. A wooden observation tower was flown in and set up in the center of the base. The ground was so hard that we used C4 plastic explosive to loosen it enough to dig our bunkers and fill the sand bags. RPG wire (chain link fencing) was put up in front of each bunker to prevent the RPGs from scoring a direct hit on the bunkers. The bunkers were each equipped with an M60 machine gun. Howitzers were airlifted in the newly established perimeter. By nightfall, we were exhausted and ready to take a break. A little after midnight, our break was cut short.

The NVA had been watching us. Our position in the middle of nowhere posed a direct challenge to their command of this swath of countryside. So they came at us all night. Mortars, RPGs, sappers, AKs, light (and heavy) machine guns. They were on the offensive in the open and we were well entrenched in our defensive positions. Our firepower was too great for them to overcome. We caught them in the open with artillery, mortars, and gunships. As it turned out, this was the plan. It was a great plan, unless you had to be on the ground putting it into action. We held them off the first night, and they came back the next night in smaller numbers. Again they were no match for our firepower. We had one KIA at Diamond II. The NVA had more.

Things were quiet for a few days. I was thinking that maybe I wouldn't see too many more nights like the first week of April. We tore down Diamond II on April 14th and moved a little closer to the enemy again. It was to build Diamond III. Same drill was followed. Bust your ass and dig your bunker. You knew that they were coming to get you again. Shortly after midnight, their intentions were made known. Alpha company took their biggest losses that night. Our LP with Michael Harr, Willie Jacobs, Ralph Maynard, and Peter Rasmussen was over run. I can still hear their radio request to come in while they could. A major (who I'll not name) denied their request to return to the perimeter. The other LPs did make it in safely. A direct hit on the mortar platoon, took out three close friends, Jimmy Lester, Stan Carter and Larry Keller. Again we were able to prevail with our tenacity and superior firepower.

I was getting short and I was looking for an opportunity to make it home intact. Suddenly it came to me. Because of the way career noncoms and officers came and went, there was no institutional memory in the company. When a new first sergeant or officer came on board, he asked the guys who were already there, how things worked in the company. When the company resupply sergeant DEROS'd, I said that it was customary for the senior RTO to take over resupply duties in the field. Although not entirely true, it worked. So I became the soda sarge for the remainder of my tour. It was great duty. Order beer, sodas, C rations, inventory ammo, pass out the mail and divide the sundry packs that contained cigarettes, candy and toiletries. Getting coffee for the first sergeant was also one of my duties. I still smile when I think of Top shouting, "Hinton, coffee ASAP!" It sure beat humping with the shoot here sign strapped to my back.

May, June and I'll be out of this place!

May

We got a new CO. He was very confident and went by the book. This was his second tour. I don't think he was in the infantry for his first tour. He didn't ask how things worked. He let you know how he wanted them to work. He was the boss and gave the orders. I was glad that I wasn't carrying the radio any longer. Anyhow, we got along okay. I followed orders and did my duties as efficiently and cheerfully as possible.

On May 26th, we were sent to set up a company perimeter in HauNghia province. The site selected was a clearing surrounded by bamboo growing on top of berms that were about the height of a man maybe 5-6ft high. It looked like it was a great defensive position against a ground attack. As we scouted the location, I found a trash pit in the center of the site. Contents were C ration tins, empty cigarette packs. Most worrisome were the mortar tail fins that were in the pit. I didn't know who had been here before, but I had a strong feeling that this was not the place for the company to set up. I took my concerns to the CO. I told him that the VC probably had this place zeroed in. He wasn't too concerned about my observation nor digging a bunker with overhead cover for one night. Willie Hackett and I decided we were too short to not have a bunker. So we chopped down bamboo and dug a bunker.

In the early hours of May 27th, we were rocketed and mortared. The RTO for the forward observer was wounded. The CO was killed. We dug a bunker and spent one night there. He didn't dig a bunker and spent the rest of his life there. It was sad. His wife's first husband had been killed in Vietnam. Now her second husband had been killed in the war. She was widowed twice and had small children.

We dismantled the perimeter and choppered to CuChi to wait for the assignment of a new CO for Alpha Company. While we were there, we had a stand down.

I was too short for this. I needed to get away before I couldn't get away. After all, I was going home at the end next month. I intended to get home in one piece.

June

I was able to get a five-day leave to Camp Zama in Japan to get my eye examined. Eye was okay. I went to Tokyo. Had to be back to Zama in time to catch the plane to the war. Walked around. Took in some shows. Had a few drinks. Rode the subway. Even though the exchange rate was 360 yen to the Dollar, I couldn't do too much because, I only had $40 in my pocket. I managed to call home and talk to my wife. It was so wonderful to hear her voice. In less than a month I would actually be home with her. I could hardly wait. To go home I had to go back to the war and finish my tour.

When I got back Cu Chi, I checked in with the Company XO, Lt. Ronnnie Jones. He knew I was short. When the first sergeant learned that I was back in country, he wanted me back in the field. LT. Jones told Top that he needed me in Cu Chi. So I did details for my last couple of weeks in country. I volunteered for KP, but they didn't need me. I found that not many people wanted to burn shit. So I volunteered to do just that. It was hot and nasty. Pour the diesel fuel in the sawed off drum. Stir it up. Light a toilet paper fuse. Keep stirring until it's reduced to ash. Other than the smell, there's not much to it. It sure beats the hell out of being shot at!

Finally my orders came for going home. I packed up and quietly bid farewell to nobody in particular. I came by myself and went by myself. On the way to the airstrip, I found a jungle hat along side the road. I didn't want to miss the plane to Long Binh, so I put the hat into my duffle bag. After about 40 years, the hat was reunited with its owner, Bob Castona.

While I was waiting for my flight back to the world, I ran into Larry Bailey. I went to high school with him and his brother, Derwin. Larry was heading back home also. Derwin would be heading to the war after Larry got home. Derwin made it to Nam, but not home. He was KIA on September 15, 1969.

On June 27th, I caught a plane home. When it touched down in California, everyone cheered. I was home from the war and in one piece! I was able to buy a first class seat with a changeover in Chicago. I remember strutting through the airport with my CIB, Bronze Star, Army Commendation and my Vietnam service ribbons. Everyone was looking at me. I thought I must be looking exceptionally sharp. I ducked into the men's room to check out my appearance. The people were staring at me because my ribbon bar had come loose. My ribbon rack was swinging back and forth like a pendulum! I was surprised that I could still laugh about myself. I really was home.

Doug Shepherd, Ohio: Fun at Any Cost

Doug Shepherd

I must tell a couple of first hand stories here about my friend Doug "Shep" Shepherd. Good soldier, just like nearly all the rest of the guys, but leaned a little farther toward having a good time or at least a laugh or two whenever possible. It has been said many times here that the men used every excuse to laugh. I really liked Shep and he was one of the guys that, though he might not have been aware of it, kept the morale from slumping.

I don't think Shep hated officers; I don't even think he didn't respect them. He just sort of used them in a lot in some of his pranks. The remarkable thing is he was never caught, punished or reprimanded for any of it.

In January 1966, which was fairly early in the first year the 25th Division spent in Vietnam. This was before the base camp had any structures besides tents and ponchos on bamboo stakes. There arose an officer's tent somewhat towards the center of the camp but still in the 27th regiment's assigned area. Now this tent was where the officers would gather and plan the operations and the next things needed for the defense of the small, but ever growing base camp. At this time they still hadn't got a fire lane cleared around the wire (Outside ring of the camp) and most of the camp was still covered in growth of some sort from trees all the way down to, what we called on the farm, scrub brush. We hadn't found the tunnels that were networked under the entire camp yet so snipers were inside the camp nearly every day doing their work. Therefore the need to have someone walk guard around this tent just in case sappers would take a stab at attacking one of those meetings.

Lucky Doug Shepherd drew a position on that guard post roster. All of us that had already served with him in Hawaii for a few months knew this would be something to keep an eye on. Sparks were sure to fly with Shep working for and so close to the officers. As he walked around and around ever so slowly and so soldier-like circling the tent as he passed the door/tent opening he pulled the pin on a smoke grenade and lifted the side of the tent just high enough to slide it under. He quickly ran to the back side of the tent. As everyone in the tent ran for clear air one of them yelled "GUARD!"

"Yes sir," came from Shep. Shep ran around to the gathering and they asked him if he had seen anyone in the area. After he made his reply of "No sir" (which was not a lie) they told him to continue. Me and the half dozen or so witnesses to this event disappeared in an instant each carrying with them this great secret.

Along about the same time period in early 66, some of our company men had constructed a makeshift shower in our area. This thing was terrible to look at but it was indeed a shower. It was an old fuel tank mounted on top of a 2x4, 4 posted affair with a poncho wrapped around it for privacy. It worked great with a buddy pouring water in the top and with those small holes punched in the bottom for a shower "head" it was much better than nothing.

We had only one officer that wanted and requested to be saluted. All the rest did not for obvious reasons. One afternoon that particular LT was in the shower when one of our snipers that harassed us daily, took a shot at the shower and the round zipped through and through the poncho barely missing the LT. He came out of the little makeshift structure like a shot and was on all fours doing sort of a cross between monkey crawling crossed with a low crawl, all this with bare back side shining. He was quickly making his way to one of the closest holes in the area dug in case of our frequent mortar attacks. Right past Shep he goes and at that time Shep put up a perfect salute toward LT and then ran alongside of LT all the 20 or 30 yards to the targeted hole in the ground. Shep was holding his salute the whole way! Of course Lt didn't know his rear was being saluted or even knew Shep was running right beside him, but he did hear a few of us laughing and thought we were making fun of him for being shot at. So we got chewed a little and Shep got away unscathed... again!

Doug Shepherd is a great example of the guys always in our mist that helped keep some sense of sanity in an insane place. Very good soldiers that could find humor in absolutely anything were a blessing and I imagine every unit in the war had at least one of them. We were lucky enough to have several of them.

Harry Davis, Crossing the River

Harry Davis is really quite a guy. He loves to visit and is very easy to talk to. A fun guy with lots of stories. He is another one of those slow talking fast thinking Tennessee boys that all possess quick wit and humor. Here in his words is Harry's story about crossing the river.

I was an RTO for "C" Company, 1 / 27 Wolfhounds and our CO was Capt. Trimble and I was his RTO. We were on a mission to try and cut the Viet Cong supply lines.

It was a typical day like all the rest, hot humid (without the rain) as we were crossing the river (not sure what river) the "Old Man" Ltc. Ernest F. Condina called from his chopper, "Mustang Charley 6, this is Mustang 6 request SIT-RAP over."

Being a young 19 year old (and was taught in commo school, "Tell It Like It Is and get off the air.") My reply was "This is Mustang Charley 65 SIT - RAP----- Alpha Sierra, Sierra Whole Deep In Water! OVER." There was a pause, the mike keyed, unkeyed, keyed up again, in a half laugh a reply "RODGER OUT!"

After the Col. landed in a safe area the Captain went over to talk about the game plain, the first thing the Col. ask was "Where Did You Get That RTO?"

The captain told him, “Oh! That's Davis,” so he called me over to meet “The Old Man,” LTC. Condina, one of the greatest men I ever knew, but before I sometimes wished I could get him down here and I would go up there.

Later before my rotation time I was asked if I would like to be the “Old Man's” RTO, I said Yes and moved to HHQ where I spent the rest of my time, I really thought I had it made, getting to fly around with the “Old Man.” DAAAA Fool! You get shot at up there too. WHAT WAS I THINKING?

Oh well, everything went ok but I sure did miss my buddies in the company, there was Craig “Dutch” De Feyter, Jim “Hack” Hackney, George Pasick, Ray Radcliffe, Rosco Burgdoll, Jimmy Richards, James Bullock, and the rest of the bunch, but the guys I served with were all worth being called Brothers, Thanks to each and every one of you and God Bless.

Harry L. Davis Jr.
C Co. 1 / 27th WOLFHOUNDS "FOREVER"

The Perimeter

A friend of mine named Jimmy Lawson wrote the following piece and I included it in my first book because it comes the closest of anything I've read to describe the feelings of almost every Vietnam veteran. Paul E. Gaither, Jr. (known as Gabby) told me after reading the book that "The Perimeter" could be put between two hard backs and be a book of its own because it said so much. I must include it in this project as well.

The Perimeter

The Perimeter, in the infantry, is a circle of men. It is half a squad, platoon or company. One half is on guard, staying vigilant, watching for the enemy, while the other half rests, sleeps and carries on with life as it is.

They are more than just men; they are a brotherhood in uniform.

They share their plans, dreams and hopes with each other. In hard times, they share their sadness, fears and pain. They face the enemy together, some like brothers, others like fathers and sons, and always as true friends. They find a spirit in each other than binds them to one another in a bond that lasts forever.

As time passes, they will leave the service and each other. They will travel many different paths of life, some to prosper well and others not so well.

Somewhere in life's travels, these men find themselves lost in the world, confused, dazed, scared, unhappy and searching for something; something they are not even sure exists. They are not soldiers anymore, they are called veterans. Somehow, in their search, they once again find others like themselves. They find brothers of the past, brothers of the Perimeter, that circle of safety, where someone else shares their pain, their confusion and their fear.

That Perimeter where that fear is eased, where there is less confusion. They share each other's pain in stories, in tears and in silence. Inside the Perimeter, eye contact can say it all.

This Perimeter is a circle of life and a circle of death; it is a circle of wounded warriors, with wounds of both flesh and spirit. This Perimeter is a circle of iron that has never broken. It is a circle of common duty that knows no color, no creed and no religious ground. The circle will last forever, through the best of times and the worst of times. The Perimeter is a place warriors will always seek - even for eternity. Just gaze out at our national cemeteries. For out there, on the outer edge, ever so vigilant, are those on the Perimeter.

By James R. Lawson
VA Medical Center - Mountain Home, Tenn.

An Understanding: The Why of It

Here, we Wolfhounds are setting up of one of the many, many temporary perimeters as James Lawson so masterfully explains.

Well, that's all the stories I'll use this time. I know that nearly all the folks that read these stories that men told to me will be Vietnam veterans. Of those, probably a large number will be members of the Wolfhounds. For those readers that aren't Vietnam Veterans, I hope these tales give you a little better understanding of what life was like for the thousands of soldiers that were there. Please understand that all but a few of them came back to a Nation that at the worst, hated them and the war. At the very best, they came back to a nation that gave them little respect or honor.

Actually, it wasn't entirely their fault they felt that way. I say that because I was among the very first to come home as I was in Vietnam at the beginning of the big escalation and with the 25th Division when they landed in Vietnam in January of 1966. Being back in the world (as we called it) so early, I was home for the rest of the war. I started watching the news, straining to see any news of my old unit. Maybe looking for a glimpse of my brothers. But what I saw wasn't what I had just left. I was watching a slanted, twisted news man's version of what I had just left. They were leaving out all the sense of compassion that I witnessed from the American Soldiers. They were leaving out the thought or idea that it was for democracy and independence of a nation fighting a Communist takeover. I saw film clips of terrible things and found out it was actually deeds by the enemy or ARVN soldiers. Bombarded with this every night, it is easy to understand the movement demanding an end to the war. But, the part that cannot be explained is what made the American people despise the soldier, many of them draftees, sent there to do a job that their country ask of them.

I tried to use a varied collection of tales here. Usually one or two events from an individual, all the time knowing that each soldier could write a complete book of his own. In some cases it was nearly impossible to get even the one tidbit. Some of my friends that I really knew their story and I wanted something from just couldn't do it for me. I understand completely. I need everyone to know that most of these men that gave me the details of an event in their life did so with great struggle. Most of the stories have not been told before except to those folks that they knew "were there." Most Vietnam Vets simply will not get into an exchange with someone about the war if the other person or group wasn't there and would not understand. That may come from the attitude that existed way back in the 70's when any discussion about the war quickly turned ugly. I know I always walked away if a group started up with that topic. And I never, ever talked to college kids from that time period. They already thought they knew everything about the war because they had television and those professors.

There are thousands of tales out there, hidden away in the minds of those brave veterans. I want to compile another collection of them if I live long enough. I believe the stories need to be told for a multitude of reasons. I'll give you a quick example to explain a big reason why the stories should be told.

The pictures I took in Vietnam are on my web site, and on the web site of a great Wolfhound friend of mine that lives in California, named William "Easy" Smith. Easy called and said he needed a copy of my first book, **See the Dragon**. *He explained to me that a young 12 year boy in Tennessee had contacted him. Easy wanted to send this young man a copy because he knew it* *had stories in it that included this young man's grandpa. Somehow the young man had stumbled on to Easy's site and told Easy that he had seen lots of pictures of his grandpa on the site. He had also seen many photos of his grandpa in Don Arndt's album that was attached to the site. The boy's name was Jaryd Campbell! That is the grandson of one of the best friends I ever had, Larry "Cam" Campbell. Now I am in contact with Jaryd and his parents. Of course the boy had never heard of anything his grandpa did because grandpa didn't talk about it. This young man has now read* ***See the Dragon*** *and the chapter about his grandpa and is so proud of him. I believe just one thing like this makes the effort worth the trouble.*

By reading about the men I know and those I knew as boys while they were becoming men, I hope you learned a little history that you didn't know before. May God always bless those that ran ***Into the Dragon's Roar****.*

Glossary

106: 106 MM Recoilless rifle, fired a large HE rocket
AO: Area of operations
AP: Ambush patrol
ARVN: Army of Republic of Vietnam
Brass: Slang term to describe Officers in charge
C 4: High explosive, like putty
C rations: Boxed meals
CIB: Combat Infantry Badge
Claymore: Command detonated mine:
Click: 1000 meters, a little over a half mile (.6)
CO: Commanding Officer
CSM: Command Sergeant Major
DEROS: Date of estimated return overseas
DI: Drill Instructor
Dust Off: Huey helicopter used as a Med Evac ambulance
E 3, E 4: E stands for enlisted, number is rank. Can be draftee or volunteer
EM: Enlisted Men
First Hounds: Meaning the First Battalion of the 27th Wolfhounds
FO: Forward Observer
FNG: Describing any new personnel. Ask any Vietnam veteran for the acronym
FSB: Forward support battalion
Gun Ship: Huey helicopter, heavily armed
H and I: Harassment and Interdiction artillery fire
HE: High Explosive
Hooch: Simple living quarters, anything from a poncho on stakes to a structure.
Humping: Infantry man's slag for walking carrying weapons and gear
Intel: Slag used to describe "reports from intelligence"
KIA: Killed in Action

KP: Kitchen Police (Mess hall slaves)
LT: Slang for Lieutenant
LP: Listening post
LZ: Landing Zone
M 79: Grenade launcher
Mini Gun: Multi-barreled machine gun
MIA: Missing In Action
MOS: Military Occupation Specialty (Job)
M 60: Belt fed machine gun
Non-Com: Slang for Non commissioned officer or Sergeant
NCO: Non Commissioned Officer
NVA: North Vietnamese Army
Platoon: Approximately 40 men
PTSD: Post Traumatic Stress Disorder
R&R: Rest and Relaxation. A week away from the war.
RTO: Radio Telephone Operator, Usually a man who carried a radio on his back
PRC 25: Two way radio
Puff: Puff the Magic Dragon. C47 plane converted to a heavily armed gun ship
PX: Post Exchange or a soldier's store
Sapper: Special Commando type soldiers. The Vietnamese called them "dac cong" meaning special task. Highly trained with explosives.
Slick: Huey helicopter used as troop carriers. M 60 machine door guns
Spooky: Also called "Puff the Magic Dragon. Converted C47 plane
Squad: Approximately 11 men
Top: Top Kick. Sergeant in charge of a Company. Highest ranking NCO
VC: Viet Cong
WIA: Wounded In Action
Wire: The "Wire" was the term given to the perimeter of camps Referring to the wire that encircled it.
XO: Executive officer

www.ingramcontent.com/pod-product-compliance
Ingram Content Group UK Ltd.
Pitfield, Milton Keynes, MK11 3LW, UK
UKHW041948190726
13854UKWH00004B/1857